Followers Making Followers

Ed

Thanks to you + Lou for helping me follow Jesus!

Steve Ridgell

ISBN: 978-0-89098-881-7

2809 12th Ave S, Nashville, TN 37204

Cover design by Jonathan Edelhuber

Table of Contents

DEDICATION

To my wife, Marsha—my partner for over forty years in making followers.

To my children: Julie Gilbreth and Joe Don and Jamie Ridgell. You live your faith, you serve others in the name of Jesus, and you share your faith.

To my Grandkids: Anna, Jake, Avery, Andrew, and Austin. More than anything, Mimi and Pops want you to follow Jesus...and help others do the same.

To my fellow disciple makers at Hope for Life. Thank you Tim Archer, Juan Monroy, Tony Fernandez, Moses Khombe-Banda, and Bruno Valle. It is my honor and my joy to work together making disciples.

ACKNOWLEDGEMENTS

I have been blessed to travel all over the world encouraging followers to live as Great Commission Christians. In doing so, I have met hundreds of people passionate about sharing their faith. I am thankful and inspired by those I have met who are making a difference in our world.

I want to say a special thanks to Bill Brant, President and CEO of Hope for Life, a Herald of Truth ministry. Bill has been a boss and a brother through this process. His encouragement and suggestions have been invaluable to me.

And thanks to Patty Brant for the outstanding work she has done as a proofreader. I appreciate it.

Thanks to the Board of Directors at Hope for Life. They consistently encourage and support me, both financially and spiritually.

Thanks to Tom Tignor and Stacey Owens of 21st Century Christian. Your partnership and encouragement are appreciated.

I am so thankful for the people whose stories are written in this book. I am renewed in my commitment to share Jesus because we have shared life together. Thanks for those who inspire me by your commitment to share Jesus. Thanks for the seekers who have found Jesus. You remind me that God is still bringing souls to Him every day.

Thank You, Jesus, for saving me and letting me partner with You in sharing the greatest news ever.

And Jesus came and said to them, "All authority in heaven and on earth has been given to me. Go therefore and make disciples of all nations, baptizing them in the name of the Father and of the Son and of the Holy Spirit, teaching them to observe all that I have commanded you. And behold, I am with you always, to the end of the age"
(Matthew 28:18-20).

Let's do this.

INTRODUCTION

It is still one of the greatest experiences of my life. I was with my Hope for Life team conducting an evangelistic event in Mozambique, excited to see firsthand the approach they were using to share the story of Jesus. We were going to host a movie night in a large park. Many people in that part of Mozambique had never seen a movie, so there was a built-in attraction. The movie being shown was *The Passion of the Christ* with subtitles in the local dialect. There would be Jesus stories told before the movie, during intermission, and after the showing.

I was curious about some of the details. For instance, what would we do if it rained? I was told we would get wet. Well, of course. I was also given instructions what to do if I spotted a Green Mamba, a highly poisonous snake. I was told to freeze and not to move. I was assured that I could not outrun or avoid being bitten, so the best plan was to hope it would slither on by. So I asked what happened if one of us were bitten.

"We die and get to go home."

But they were good to me. They even let me stay in the guest house. I assured them that even though I looked like I was too old, I could still stay in a tent if needed. But they convinced me to accept their hospitality by telling me the guest house had a bathroom and running water.

There was a bathroom. It was just that nothing in it worked the way I thought. And there was running water. Every morning about 6:00, a young man went down to the river, filled a bucket with water, ran up the stairs to our room, and announced: "Running water." Ha ha.

But the night of the event was amazing. There was a huge crowd of around 4,000. About half of the crowd was clearly Muslim. But they watched the movie and heard the stories of Jesus. At the end of the presentation, we invited people to come meet with our team if they wanted to be baptized or if they wanted to learn more about Jesus. Hundreds of people began to make their way toward us. And it was at that point that many of the Muslims began to run interference. It was never violent. I never felt threatened. But they clearly came between our team and the people attempting to meet with us. We literally resorted to announcing over the microphone that if anyone wanted to know more about Jesus that they should find a member of their local church of Christ.

And Here Is What Happened Next...

Only four young men made it through that human barrier to talk to our team. When asked what we could do for them, they said they were ready to die with Jesus in baptism and be raised to a new life. So about 100 Christians set off on a one-mile hike to the nearest water to witness their new birth. Once we got there, a couple of the men waded into the water and began to beat the surface with their hands. I asked Moses Banda, our team leader, if we should be helping with whatever it was they were doing. He laughed and told me to go ahead. He then explained they were making sure there were no crocodiles nearby. I declined to help, feeling a little guilty for being glad I was not the one doing the baptizing.

After the baptisms, we all went to enjoy a fellowship meal. One of the local chiefs had donated a cow so we could feed the church members. The new Christians and some of our team leaders were honored by being the first to eat and by being allowed to eat inside. We were served the liver, which I was assured was a great honor. I happen to like beef liver, though I have to admit I would have been more excited had they done more with it than simply walk it by the fire.

They asked if I would talk to our new brothers about what to do as new Christians. So for a couple of hours, we visited about what Jesus expected of them as His followers. We talked about living as forgiven people, about serving others in the name of Jesus, and about speaking boldly the good news of Jesus to their family and friends. They returned to their villages, and I flew back to the States. One year later, Moses Banda returned to Mozambique to see what had happened to our young brothers and to find out if any of those turned away had ever made contact with local Christians.

And...

Those four young men had all gone back to their villages and started sharing the gospel. Many of those who could not connect with our team the night of the campaign later found Christians who shared Jesus with them. The new Christians talked to their family and friends.

And now there are 150 new congregations ranging in size from 50–400. The good news had exploded all over that part of Mozambique.

You may be saying to yourself: *But that was then and there. Not here and now.* So can the same thing happen in your world today?

And if not...then why not?

That is what this book is about. It is about followers of Jesus going into their world to make more followers.

Because Jesus said...

> ***All authority in heaven and on earth has been given to me. Go therefore and make disciples of all nations, baptizing them in the name of the Father and of the Son and of the Holy Spirit, teaching them to observe all that I have commanded you. And behold, I am with you always, to the end of the age.***
>
> Matthew 28:18-20

Big Fish and Lost Worms

It was the fishing experience of a lifetime. My son, Joe Don, and I got to spend three days fishing for black bass on El Salto Lake in Mexico. It was a birthday/Christmas/anniversary gift from our wives. We spent all day on the lake fishing, and at night, we would gather in a dining hall and eat with all the others fishing with the same guide service.

Every night, we realized we were catching lots more fish than everyone else. We also found out we were catching bigger fish than anyone else. We learned one other thing. We were losing more plastic worms than everyone else. And we realized something else: These were connected. The big fish, and the big numbers of fish, were in places that were hard to get to and difficult to cast into. So we sometimes hung up our worms and had to break them off. But we were putting our bait where the fish were.

Big fish and lost worms.

And it reminded me of what Jesus did.

For the Son of Man came to seek and to save the lost.
Luke 19:10

Jesus came to this earth because that is where the sinners were. And still are. It was so different from heaven and the constant worship of angels. He came right into our messy, dirty, sinful lives and died on a cross for our sins. So He could save us.

Our world is full of people who need Jesus. Your world is full of people who need the good news of Jesus.

So we go into our world to share the Jesus we follow. Our world needs what we have.

We live as followers, who make followers, who make followers... of Jesus.

CHAPTER 1

IT IS ALWAYS ABOUT JESUS

Let me be absolutely clear about one thing. We are Jesus followers committed to making more Jesus followers. Sometimes we get so caught up in the who, what, where, when, and how of making disciples that we lose sight of the main thing. And the main thing is Jesus. The Great Commission in Matthew 28 starts with the assertion that Jesus has all authority on earth and in heaven. He is the one in charge. We are making disciples of Jesus.

Not disciples of a church, or a doctrine, or a lifestyle—but followers of Jesus. The good news we share with others is Jesus. The message we carry into our world is Jesus. We are making Jesus followers because that is who we are, and that is what He told us to do.

So keep the main thing the main thing.

Jesus: The Way, The Truth, The Life

If you are not talking about Jesus, you are not making disciples. Well, not Jesus disciples anyway. Jesus Himself said...

> ***I am the way and the truth and the life. No one comes to the Father except through me.***
> John 14:6

Jesus is the way, the only way to God. I sometimes hear people talk about the Great Commission, and it seems as if they skip right past Jesus. For example, some people emphasize baptism so much that it seems as if they are teaching that it is the way to God. Yes, baptism is clearly part of disciple-making. Jesus says that. But talking about how to follow Jesus is not the same as talking about Jesus. If you misplace the emphasis, you will end up with a bunch of wet people who do not follow Jesus. And you end up with churches that baptize almost every one of their children as they grow up, yet wonder why so many of them end up not following Jesus when they leave home.

And...you are not the way to God. Nor is the church the way to God.

Jesus is the way. The only way to God.

Jesus is the truth. Some might make obeying the teaching of Jesus the main emphasis of disciple-making. Sometimes that emphasis is so misplaced that churches give the impression Christianity is about following a set of dos and don'ts instead of following Jesus. And if not careful, you forget why you live the way you do. You end up fighting over the rules, making new rules, and reducing Christianity to a series of acts to do—or not do. Disciples follow Jesus, not rules. The truth is not found in correct doctrine or theology. There are beliefs that are true, but they are not the truth. Jesus is. We do not want to make disciples of doctrine or commands.

Becoming a disciple is about Jesus. How to become a disciple or how to live as a disciple is important, but they are not the same as Jesus. He is the focus of making followers. Not followers of commands or doctrine, but followers of Jesus. Life is only found in Jesus. Eternal life with God is only found in Jesus.

Jesus is the way. Jesus is the truth. Jesus is the life. And only Jesus.

Follow Him. Make other followers of Jesus.

Peter, a follower of Jesus, explained it this way in one of his sermons. While speaking about healing a cripple in the name of Jesus Christ, he said...

> ***And there is salvation in no one else, for there is no other name under heaven given among men by which we must be saved.***
> Acts 4:12

Making disciples always starts with the good news of Jesus. There is no other message that matters as much as the Jesus story.

And the Jesus Message Is Good News

So what exactly does one have to know about Jesus to be His follower? There are prophecies about Jesus all through the Old Testament. The four Gospels are full of stories and sayings from Jesus. There is Jesus information right up through the end of the book of Revelation. The Apostle John ends his Gospel by reminding us that if everything Jesus did had been written down, then even the entire world could not hold the books. So what is the most important thing to know about Jesus?

Paul answers this question for us in 1 Corinthians 15.

> ***Now I would remind you, brothers, of the gospel I preached to you, which you received, in which you stand, and by which you are being saved, if you hold fast to the word I preached to you—unless you believed in vain.***
>
> ***For I delivered to you as of first importance what I also received:***
> 1 Corinthians 15:1-3

Paul is reminding the Corinthian church of vital information. Here are the various ways he identifies this information:

1. It is good news. The word Paul uses is *gospel*, but the meaning is good news. This information is something that brings joy.
2. Paul preached these facts. He is reminding them of the message he shared with them. The story of Paul's time in Corinth is told in Acts 18. Paul spent his time testifying that Jesus was the Christ. He stayed there for eighteen months, and many Corinthians believed this message and were baptized.
3. This good news is what they believed. It is what led them to respond to Jesus and become His followers.

4. It is the truth on which they stand. It is their worldview. It is the truth upon which they have based their lives.
5. It is the good news that saves them. And it will continue to save them as long as they continue to believe it.
6. This good news gospel is of first importance. If there was any doubt about how important this information really is, Paul makes it clear. This is of first importance. It is the main thing to know about Jesus.

...that Christ died for our sins in accordance with the Scriptures, that he was buried, that he was raised on the third day in accordance with the Scriptures...

1 Corinthians 15:3-4

There it is. The truth about Jesus that people must know. The most important thing to know about Jesus. Jesus died for our sins. That is the good news. Because God loved us so much that He would send His Son to die for our sins. For my sins and for your sins. For the sins of my friends, my family, my world. That is the message.

And it is real. They buried Jesus in a tomb. That is what you do with dead people. You bury them. That leads to the rest of the greatest news our world can ever hear...

God raised Jesus from the dead on the third day, just like the Scripture says. Jesus not only died for our sins, but He was raised from the dead and now lives in heaven with God.

So can we. And that is the message our world needs to hear. That is the good news for a lost world. That is the news that can lead people to become followers of Jesus. It is why you are a follower of Jesus.

So We Connect People To Jesus

We want to be like the Apostle Andrew, who spent his life connecting people to Jesus. Andrew was a disciple of John and was eagerly looking to find the Messiah. That story is recorded in John 1:35-42. John pointed to Jesus as the lamb of God, so Andrew and another one of John's disciples immediately left John and followed Jesus. They spent the day with Jesus learning that He was, in fact, the Christ.

And the first thing Andrew did after he left Jesus was to find his brother, Simon, and tell him the good news of Jesus.

> ***He brought him to Jesus.***
> John 1:42

Simon might never have known Jesus if not for his brother, Andrew. Andrew became a disciple and went into his world to make other disciples. By the way, you may know Simon by the name Jesus gave him—Peter. Simon Peter was the leader of the apostles, the main speaker on Pentecost, and perhaps the most powerful preacher in the early days of the church. But if not for Andrew, you might never have heard of Peter.

Or of This Miracle

Almost every Christian I know can tell the story of the feeding of the 5,000 in John 6:1-13. It is an amazing story: a multitude of hungry people, no place to buy food, and no money even if there were a place. The disciples had no idea what to do. Then a young boy showed up to offer Jesus his five loaves and two small fish. I can only imagine the faith and courage it took to approach this group of men around Jesus. Perhaps he stood there hoping someone would notice him. Or maybe he was searching for a friendly face, someone who could help him with his offering.

It was Andrew who saw him. Or maybe Andrew was the one the boy approached. And the boy said to Andrew that he wanted to share his meager meal with others. So in the midst of this frantic discussion among the disciples about how to feed this multitude, Andrew spoke up.

> ***"There is a boy here who has five barley loaves and two fish, but what are they for so many?"***
> John 6:9

It is clear Andrew does not know what Jesus would do with this gift, but he knew enough to connect this young boy to Jesus. Jesus gave thanks, and God multiplied the loaves and fishes, and 5,000 people got all they could eat with plenty left over. It's an amazing story that happened because of Jesus, a young boy with great faith,—and Andrew, who knew to connect people with the Savior.

And What About These Greeks?

What do you do if you are an outsider trying to get to Jesus? You are a group of Greeks among a multitude of worshiping Jews. But you want to see Jesus. So you approach Phillip. Maybe it was because his name was Greek, or maybe he was the first apostle they could find. But they told Phillip they wanted to see Jesus. I am not sure Phillip knew what to do with these "outsiders." So he told Andrew. Did he choose Andrew because of his wisdom? Or did he seek out Andrew because Andrew was known as a facilitator for people seeking Jesus? And Andrew did exactly what you would expect him to do—he took Phillip and they told Jesus.

Andrew connected people to Jesus: his brother, a young boy, a group of Greeks. He got it. Andrew followed Jesus. And he helped others get to Jesus. A follower who made followers. A disciple who lived in his world and connected people to Jesus.

CHAPTER 2

IT IS ABOUT MAKING FOLLOWERS OF JESUS

It is a call to action. As a follower of Jesus, you are called to make other followers. To make a follower is to share the good news of Jesus with others and to invite them to be His disciple. It is to teach, guide, and walk with those who decide to accept that invitation to be a follower of Jesus.

But you do not make other disciples just by doing things Jesus would do. That makes you a disciple. To feed the hungry, to be friends with the lonely, and to assist the poor are things Jesus would—and did—do. However, to make a disciple means we must tell the reason we do those things. We must point to Jesus and to God with our service. To be like Jesus and not tell others how they, too, can follow Him borders on cruelty. How can you claim to love someone while teasing them with this glimpse of a different life and then not share how they, too, can have this life?

So You Have Something To Do... and To Say

You have a calling, a mission, a job to do. You are to represent Jesus in this world. You are driven to share the message that changed your life. The Apostle Paul wrote about this in 2 Corinthians.

> ***For Christ's love controls us, because we have concluded this: that one has died for all, therefore all have died; and he died for all, that those who live might no longer live for themselves but for him who for their sake died and was raised.***
>
> 2 Corinthians 5:14-15

We believers have given our lives to Jesus. We are absolutely convinced that Jesus died for each of the people with whom we connect every day in our world. This act of love is the driving force in how we now live. We are motivated, inspired, and compelled by the love Jesus showed for us when He died for our sins.

And this changes everything.

We See People Differently

> ***From now on, therefore, we regard no one according to the flesh. Even though we once regarded Christ according to the flesh, we regard him this way no longer. Therefore, if anyone is in Christ, he is a new creation, The old has passed away; behold the new has come.***
> 2 Corinthians 5:16-17

We view the world through Jesus' eyes. We do not see simply a waitress serving meals in a restaurant, just a salesman at the mall, a neighbor across the street, or a parent at the Little League field. These are people who God loves and for whom Jesus died. That changes everything about how we see people, treat people, and relate to people. We see an old world waiting to be made new. Jesus made us into a new creation. He longs to do the same for the people in our world.

So Our People Are Our Ministry

Some may see that last statement and immediately respond that the people around us are not merely targets to be converted. Correct. God does not see them that way, and neither do we. You do not let your son die for someone unless you love that person very much. Jesus loved people so much that He died so they could be made new. So we do not see people merely as conversion opportunities, but as people Jesus died to save. We look at them with eyes of love... just like Jesus does.

But they are our purpose and our reason for being in this world. They are our ministry. The people in your world are your ministry.

All this is from God, who through Christ reconciled us to himself and gave us the ministry of reconciliation: that is, in Christ God was reconciling the world to himself, not counting their trespasses against them, and entrusting to us the message of reconciliation.
2 Corinthians 5:18-19

This is God's plan. He sent Jesus, and through Him we have been reconciled—brought back together—to God. Our sins are no longer counted against us. That is news that changes my life every day. I am one with God in spite of my failings, my shortcomings, my sin. Thank You, Jesus.

But I cannot keep this good news to myself. I have heard people say that salvation is like winning a million dollars, and so, of course, we would tell everyone our good news. This is not exactly correct. The better analogy would be that we won a million dollars and found out that everyone else we knew could, too. Then it becomes more than just sharing our good news. It is sharing our good news and informing them that they, too, have good news. Living with God forever is worth so much more than anything this world has to offer. And we have it. So can everyone else.

God gave us the responsibility to get the word out. Everyone can be reconciled to God. Their sins never have to be counted against them. But they must hear this amazing news. And God gave us the job of sharing the good news that man can be reconciled to God. We have this ministry of reconciliation.

So Go Into Your World and Represent Jesus

God loved this world enough that He let His Son die so that our sins would not be counted against us. That is good news for every person you see today. Every one. But many of them have no idea. More than anything they need to hear this message from God. God's decision on how to get the word out was simple: Send His people into His world to tell others.

> ***Therefore, we are ambassadors for Christ, God making his appeal through us. We implore you on behalf of Christ, be reconciled to God.***
> 2 Corinthians 5:20

You carry the message of God into your world. It is communicated by the way you live, by how you serve others, and by what you say to them. Every day you represent Christ in your home, your neighborhood, your school, and your workplace. The good news of Jesus is entrusted to you. You carry the message of reconciliation into restaurants, ball fields, malls, and theaters.

Someone helped you to know Jesus. Now you are entrusted with helping the people in your world to know Him. God makes His salvation appeal through you.

Just Like He Did With Philip

Philip was deeply involved in the early days of the church in Jerusalem. In fact, when there was an issue concerning the care of some Grecian widows, Philip was one of the men selected to handle the situation. One of the men who was wise and full of the Holy Spirit. One of the other men involved was Stephen, a preacher so powerful in proclaiming Jesus as the Messiah that the Jewish leaders had him killed. This led to an intense persecution of Christians. Many believers left Jerusalem, but everywhere they went, they told the story of Jesus. They went into their world as representatives of Jesus.

Philip ended up in Samaria, and his preaching was powerful. So powerful that...

> ***...when they believed Philip as he preached good news about the kingdom of God and the name of Jesus Christ, they were baptized, both men and women.***
> Acts 8:12

Philip talked about Jesus in Jerusalem when God was adding saved people to the church every day. He preached the good news of Jesus in a city in Samaria and many believed him and were baptized. He represented Jesus by healing people and by talking about Jesus. People responded. He was a disciple making disciples.

Then one day he got a visit from an angel with an unusual request. He was told to go to the south to a desert road. Philip went. His world had just changed. No longer in Jerusalem and now no longer in a city in Samaria, but beside a desert road. Then a chariot came by. In the chariot was an important government official from Ethiopia.

The Holy Spirit then told Philip to go to the chariot. He ran to do so (don't you love that attitude of obedience). The Ethiopian was reading from his Isaiah scroll. The passage was from Isaiah 53 about an innocent lamb humiliated and killed without protesting, a lamb whose life was then taken up from the earth. Philip struck up a conversation, got invited into the chariot, and told the Ethiopian the good news of Jesus.

Philip did not see his new friend the way people of the world did. He was not concerned that he was of a different race and nationality. He was not concerned about economic status or religious knowledge. He did see him with the eyes of Jesus: a new friend who needed to know the good news that Jesus died for his sins. Philip was an ambassador for Jesus.

An angel from God told Philip to go to the desert road. The Holy Spirit told him to go to the chariot. But no one told him to talk about Jesus...because it was assumed that was what followers did. Just like us, Philip was in the disciple-making business. And to make disciples, you talk about Jesus. Philip seized the opportunity to share the message of reconciliation.

As for the Ethiopian...? He believed what Philip shared with him. He responded to the good news by being baptized into Christ. Afterward, he went on his way rejoicing because he was now a disciple. And as for Philip, the Holy Spirit caught him up and dropped him at Azotus. He then traveled around, preaching until he settled in Caesarea. Wherever he found himself, Philip talked about Jesus. That is what God's representatives do. And when Philip settled in Caesarea, his nickname was the "evangelist." He was a follower who made other followers.

It still happens today. I am convinced the Holy Spirit is still active in this world connecting believers and seekers. I believe there are people in your world—your neighborhood, your work, your school, your family—who need to know that Jesus died for their sins. And how will they hear the good news? God puts one of His representatives—you—into their world. A follower who is committed to making other followers. Someone who is living the good news of Jesus. Someone who will share that good news with the people in their world.

Someone like Philip.

And Someone Like You

And this is the place where you may be tempted to point out that you are not really like Philip. You may think you do not have the talent or the training to make followers. So here is the secret of being a disciple-maker. It is what someone observed about Peter and John, two of the apostles.

> ***Now when they saw the boldness of Peter and John, and perceived that they were uneducated, common men, they were astonished. And they recognized that they had been with Jesus.***
> Acts 4:13

It was not training and talent that made them bold and courageous in making disciples. It was their relationship with Jesus. They were ordinary men doing extraordinary things. It was easy to see they were not educated men. No university degrees in Bible for them. I doubt they had ever attended an evangelism workshop. They were just common men. Maybe they were like you and me.

But they were bold in talking about Jesus, because they had been with Him. That is what was obvious. To make followers of Jesus, you only need to do one thing: Be a follower yourself. That gives you courage. In the first part of this chapter, we looked at what Paul said about being ambassadors for God. Right before he talked about our call to share the message of reconciliation, Paul spoke of being compelled by the love of Christ.

There it is. Jesus died for you. You believed that. You became His disciple. And that relationship drives you to bring others to where you are. With Jesus.

Love Acts

Disciples do what their Master commands. Followers do what the leader says. So as disciple-makers we obey what Jesus commanded—and we teach others to do so also. Jesus said that was part of disciple making—teaching people to obey what He commanded. The last thing Jesus told His followers was to make disciples. So if we are to be disciples, then we must obey Him.

If you love me, you will keep my commandments.
John 14:15

Making disciples is not about talent, knowledge, or giftedness. It is a matter of the heart.

Do you love Jesus?

If so, you will obey His command to do whatever you can to make disciples.

CHAPTER 3

LOVE GOD

Of course, you cannot live as a disciple-maker unless you are a disciple. Jesus said disciples must learn to obey all He commanded. He said if you love Him, you would obey Him. So if you want to make disciples, you have to be obedient to Jesus' commands. Because you love Him. So far, so good. Until someone asks: Which commands? All of them? Implied commands or only those specifically stated? Do you compile a list to follow? How long does a new Christian have to learn—and then to obey—all of these commands?

It is easy to see how this process can devolve into a system of rule keeping. And we want to make followers, not just rule keepers. It can be overwhelming for a new follower of Jesus. It can be overwhelming for us.

It would be so much clearer if there were an obvious starting point; if only there were a foundational command on which to build.

And, of course, there is.

The Most Important Command

It was asked of Jesus in different ways.

"What is the most important commandment?"

"What must I do to inherit eternal life?"

"Which is the greatest commandment?"

Jesus did not answer by claiming all commands are equal. He answered their questions this way.

And you shall love the Lord your God with all your heart and with all your soul and with all your mind and with all your strength.
Mark 12:30

We must teach our friends to love God if they want to be disciples of Jesus. We must love God if we are going to be a follower of Jesus.

This command has always been the most important command for God's people. In Deuteronomy 6, the people of Israel are instructed how to teach this commandment. It can certainly serve as a blueprint for teaching disciples today.

Here are the key points:

- It is to be upon our hearts. We disciple by example, showing how to love God.
- This command is to be taught to our children. If you are a parent, the most important disciples you will make are your own children.
- Talk about this command always. When eating, when at home, when traveling. Early in the morning and late at night. That is how to make Jesus followers of your friends and neighbors. Invite them for meals, open your home, start early, and use your nights. Talk about loving God and His Hon.
- Make the command visible. I don't know that you need to put it on your hands and forehead. Or on your doorframe. But I do think you ought to keep God's Word, the Bible, central to your teaching. Have your Bible in sight. When telling Jesus stories, let your friends know how to find that story in the Bible. Give them a Bible if they don't have one.

Becoming a disciple, following Jesus, and reaching others are all love acts. We are not teaching people to keep a set of rules, nor do we want them to check off a series of acts you must do to be a Christian. We want people to love God. We are sharing a love story.

We do not want to make disciples because they are afraid. Or guilty. Or because of our logical explanations. We want to make disciples because we teach them to love God.

Being a disciple, and being a disciple maker, is a heart decision.

And if it is not…

You End Up Going to Church In Ephesus

Jesus wrote a letter to the church in Ephesus. You can read it in the first part of Revelation 2. On the surface it would seem they were a wonderful church. Jesus acknowledged that He knew what they had done, that they worked hard, and that they did not quit. They were a church that would not allow wicked men to have influence. They even tested those claiming to be apostles, but really weren't. This church had kept on keeping on even in hard times. They were still going strong.

But Jesus had a problem with this church. It was a problem so bad that He called on them to repent or they would cease to be His church. And what was this dangerous problem? They had left their first love. They were hard workers busy with kingdom business, but for the wrong reasons. They had strayed from the most important command. They were working out of duty, or guilt, or habit. But they were not working because they loved God. So they ended up a church that was just playacting in many ways: busy work, programs, organized ministries, and a heavy dose of chores for Jesus.

So what does that have to do with making followers of Jesus? You will only be effective as a disciple maker when your motivation is first and foremost because you love God. The Ephesian Christians sound like they are punching a time clock and going to work. If the only reason you are even considering how to live as a disciple maker is because you see it as a duty, or because you feel guilty if you do not, those motivations will not last. I would even suggest that your friends and neighbors will see right through you.

But when you are deeply in love with God, everything changes. I love God because He loved me and gave His Son to die for me. He loves so much that He made me part of His forever family. Then invited me to partner with Him in the work of reconciliation. Just like He loved you.

I share the good news of Jesus because I love God and Jesus with everything I have. You do, too.

So let us all love God so much that we become like this girl.

Talking About Who You Love

I cannot even imagine how she must have felt. She was a young Jewish girl captured by the Aram army. She had become a servant to the wife of the commander of that army. I would tell you her name, but I do not know what it is. Her story is found in 2 Kings 5, and it is amazing. The husband of her mistress had leprosy. His name was Naaman, and he was so successful in his career that even the king identified him as a great man. Professionally successful, great character...but a leper. Socially unacceptable, difficult for his marriage.

Naaman heard about the prophet Elisha, a man of God. He went to see Elisha in hopes that Elisha's God could heal him. It took some convincing for Naaman to have faith, but eventually he did, and he was healed from his leprosy. And he recognized that there is no God but the God of Israel.

But how did he end up visiting Elisha in the first place? It started with that anonymous young girl who loved her God. A young girl who told her mistress that she wished Naaman would visit the prophet of the God who could heal him. It is not even apparent that she was trying to convince her mistress to persuade her husband to go. It seems more to be a matter-of-fact statement of love.

Hurting for the hopelessness Naaman must have felt, aware

of the pain his wife—her mistress—must have felt. So full of love and faith in her God, she just knew that if Naaman could visit God's prophet, then he would be healed. So she shared her faith with her mistress, who then told her husband of this God. Naaman asked his king for permission to go, and it was granted. And he was healed.

Because a young girl had been raised to love her God. Because even in captivity and taken from her home, she still loved and believed in her God. And because she could not help but speak about her God.

That is how loving God works. Loving God compels us to speak. That love gives us the courage to put faith in action.

And loving God leads us...

To also love our neighbor as our self.

CHAPTER 4

LOVE YOUR NEIGHBOR AS YOURSELF

Jesus said to make disciples by teaching others to obey what He commanded. He made it clear that the most important command to teach is to love God with everything you have. It is just as clear what the next most important command is.

> ***And you shall love the Lord your God with all your heart and with all your soul and with all your mind and with all your strength.' The second is this: 'You shall love your neighbor as yourself.' There is no other commandment greater than these."***
>
> Mark 12:30-31

That young servant girl discussed in the last chapter clearly loved her God and loved her mistress. She spoke out of that love and her deep faith. Loving God drives us to obey Him. Loving our neighbor compels us to invite others into God's story.

How we treat people matters. Loving our neighbor is more than making sure we refrain from doing evil to them.

Loving your neighbor leads to action.

It did for Jesus, and it does for those who follow Him.

Loving People Means Seeing Them

Life had not been good to him. After all, he was a blind beggar. Every day, he sat by the side of the road hoping that people would have pity on him so that he could gather enough coins to buy something to eat. But one day he heard people in the crowd talking and realized they were talking about him. Or, to be more exact, they were talking about him as a case study in theology.

The disciples of Jesus were the ones talking, and the subject was about why he was born blind. Was it a result of his sin or the sin of his parents?

This story, found in John 9, is so powerful because it is so contemporary. Most of us have done exactly what they were doing. Whose fault is it that their life has turned out this way? Lonely, poor, scarred and scared, with broken relationships and broken bodies. Wondering—or assuming we know—whose fault it is. As if deciding where the fault lies will absolve us of any responsibility. It is so much easier to debate abstract theology than to actually engage with another person.

But not for Jesus. His followers saw a theological question. Jesus saw a person in pain. The disciples were missing the point. Listen to what Jesus said about this blind man.

> ***Jesus answered, "It was not that this man sinned, or his parents, but that the works of God might be displayed in him. We must work the works of him who sent me while it is day; night is coming, when no one can work. As long as I am in the world, I am the light of the world."***
>
> John 9:3-5

There are people in your world who are lost. This world is hard, and they are without hope. But God longs to do a great work in their lives. Just like He has worked in our lives. You have an amazing opportunity to share the light of this world. There is still time to work. God expects you to represent Him to the broken people in your world so that He can work to heal and to reconcile them to Himself.

Jesus saw a blind man through eyes of love. He helped him and gave him his sight. What a great story! He healed him by making mud pies for the man's eyes. The rest of the story is about this man's journey to become a disciple. It is a hard journey because Jesus does not force anyone to believe in Him. He started where this man was in his life and let him grow from there. Jesus loved him enough to serve him. And loved him enough to lead him to believe in Him as the Son of Man. The story ends with this previously blind man worshiping Jesus.

Jesus loved His neighbor. He served him by healing. He led him to belief. God did an amazing work in this man's life. He saved him. And by letting His disciples see this, He taught them to see and to love the people in their world. And He is teaching you to see and to love the people in your world.

See them, get to know them, learn their story, serve them, and share Jesus with them. Start where they are. Let God do an amazing work in their life. Because you love them. More importantly, because God loves them.

And love them enough to act radically.

What Loving Your Neighbor Looks Like

They were on their way to worship when it happened. Peter and John were asked for money by a crippled man. Peter looked him right in the eye and explained that they did not have financial resources to give, but they would give what they had. Then in the name of Jesus, they commanded the cripple to get up and walk. They then helped him up, and he began to walk and even to jump...all the while praising God.

People came from all around to see what had happened, and Peter used this opportunity to talk about Jesus. He spoke of Jesus' being crucified and raised from the dead by God. He affirmed that it was by Jesus' name and faith that the man was healed. He then called on his hearers to repent and turn to God.

So if we are going to love our neighbors as ourselves, what does this story from Acts 3 teach us about being a follower of Jesus who makes other followers?

Loving our neighbors is directly connected to loving God. They were on their way to worship when they encountered this man.

Learn to see the people in your world. Peter looked directly into his eyes to talk. See, meet, know, hear people.

Connecting to people is personal, not financial. People need us, not just our money.

Talk about Jesus. They loved this man—and helped this man—in the name of Jesus. And when healed, he praised God...not Peter and John.

They used healing as an opportunity to talk about God and Jesus. Loving your neighbor opens the door to sharing God's love with people.

And Especially Love Your Church Family

We will discuss in a later chapter how Jesus defines the neighbor you are to love as yourself. But I want to say there is a special relationship that we have with other Christians. We are family, and we especially take care of one another.

> ***So then, as we have opportunity, let us do good to everyone, and especially to those who are of the household of faith.***
> Galatians 6:10

This would seem to fall under the subject of living as a disciple, not making disciples, but I think there is something attractive about being part of a family—a community—that takes care of one another. It would be incredibly inviting if people talked about your church this way.

"Well, if anything bad ever happens, you should be a member of that church over there. They really take care of one another."

Christians do not have to depend on social services. We depend on one another. Whether it's providing food for our hungry members, sitting with sick brothers and sisters, giving furniture and clothes, or visiting the lonely, we take care of our own. People see that, and they take notice. That kind of community attracts people who want to make a difference.

That is one of the things that makes us authentic. After all, Jesus said...

By this all people will know that you are my disciples, if you have love for one another.

John 13:35

There is a priority to taking care of the people in my world. I work in order to provide for the needs of myself and my family. Then I help take care of those in my spiritual family—my church. Then I take care of those I encounter who are in need.

Followers make followers by inviting people to be a part of something greater than themselves. We make a real difference in this world. We change lives. By loving our God, loving our Jesus family, and loving those in our world.

So If I Don't Talk About Jesus...

If you do not talk to the people in your world about Jesus, it is difficult to see how you actually love them. God told you to make disciples. If you do not, what does that say about your love for God? If you know good news that can save your neighbor from his sins and you do not share that news, how is that love?

In fact, I would suggest that refusing to share the good news of Jesus with a lost and dying world would be closer to hate than to love. It is cruel at best and hateful at worst. And I do not think most of you hate the people in your world. But do you really love your neighbor as yourself?

Neglect, indifference, and apathy are the enemies of love. Love is manifested in action. I believe that most of us really do love God and love our neighbors.

So why are we not telling them about Jesus?

CHAPTER 5

SO WHY TALK ABOUT BAPTISM?

My wife and I spent a number of years ministering to, and with, university students. Two or three times a year we would get a phone call that went like this...

"Are you the person that preaches to the university students?"

"I am. Can I help you with something?"

"Yes. My daughter has never been baptized. Can you do something about that?"

"So...do you want me to baptize her, or do you want me to make her into a disciple of Jesus?"

And that is where the phone call usually ended.

Clearly baptism is important in making followers of Jesus. After all, Jesus said...

> ***Go therefore and make disciples of all nations, baptizing them in the name of the Father and of the Son and of the Holy Spirit, teaching them to observe all that I have commanded you.***
> Matthew 28:19-20

Becoming a follower of Jesus involves a conscious decision to choose Jesus. It is to refuse to follow anyone or anything else. It is to respond to God's love for us. It is love in action.

It Is to Die With Jesus

In Chapter One, I wrote about the good news message of Jesus found in 1 Corinthians 15. The most important thing to know is that Jesus died for our sins, and that God raised Him on the third day. If becoming a disciple is all about Jesus, then why does

Jesus bring up baptism? After all, we are trying to make followers of Jesus, disciples of Jesus, people who will represent Jesus in our world.

But you cannot be these things until you die.

The Apostle Paul said it like this when he was reminding the disciples in Rome of the time they were baptized.

> ***What shall we say then? Are we to continue in sin that grace may abound? By no means! How can we who died to sin still live in it? Do you not know that all of us who have been baptized into Christ Jesus were baptized into his death? We were buried therefore with him by baptism into death, in order that, just as Christ was raised from the dead by the glory of the Father, we too might walk in newness of life.***
>
> ***For if we have been united with him in a death like his, we shall certainly be united with him in a resurrection like his. We know that our old self was crucified with him in order that the body of sin might be brought to nothing, so that we would no longer be enslaved to sin. For one who has died has been set free from sin.***
>
> Romans 6:1-7

Paul was responding to the way some disciples might miss the point of being a Jesus follower. Since grace is so powerful, then to continue living a sinful life just gives grace more opportunity to increase. Paul's answer was to remind them what happened when they were baptized—when they became disciples. Followers of Jesus are baptized into Him and into His death. Baptism is being buried with Him so that we can live a new life as His disciple. To become a follower of Jesus is to die with Jesus, to die to your old life of sin, to die to yourself.

When you are united with Jesus in His death like this (baptism), then it assures you that you will be united in His resurrection from the dead. The old self is crucified, the body of sin is done away with, and we are no longer a slave to sin,.

because we died with Jesus and were freed from sin. We become His disciples and followers both now and forever.

Crucified by Grace Through Faith

Being a follower of Jesus is a choice. Making disciples is telling and showing the people in your world the good news of Jesus and inviting them to participate in it. It is dying with Jesus to live a new life as His follower. That is what baptism is, but do not misunderstand. Baptism is not just a one-time act of admission to discipleship. It is choosing a life. Here is how Paul described this dying to live.

> ***I have been crucified with Christ. It is no longer I who live, but Christ who lives in me. And the life I now live in the flesh I live by faith in the Son of God, who loved me and gave himself for me.***
>
> Galatians 2:20

This is what it means to live as a follower of Jesus. When you were baptized, you were crucified with Jesus. Your life is now lived by faith in the One who loved you and gave Himself for you when He died on the cross. That is the life into which you invite others. That is the significance of baptizing those who decide to follow Jesus.

In that same letter to the Galatians, Paul explained baptism this way...

> ***for in Christ Jesus you are all sons of God, through faith. For as many of you as were baptized into Christ have put on Christ.***
>
> Galatians 3:26 27

Baptism is a faith decision. When you were baptized into Christ, you put on Christ. Making other disciples is teaching them and inviting them to put their love and faith into action by dying to self and putting on Christ.

When we represent Jesus in our world and share His message of grace, we invite people to put their faith in the One who died for each of us. God acted in love to let Jesus die for our sins. That is saving grace. And we respond in faith.

> ***For by grace you have been saved through faith. And this is not your own doing; it is the gift of God, not a result of works, so that no one may boast. For we are his workmanship, created in Christ Jesus for good works, which God prepared beforehand, that we should walk in them.***
>
> Ephesians 2:8-10

Baptism is not something we do to save ourselves. God saves us through grace. Salvation is His free gift of love. Baptism is our response of faith to the love of God. It our surrendering of our lives so that we can partner with God in the work of reconciliation. We *make* disciples because we *are* disciples.

Baptism Is About Jesus

> ***Go therefore and make disciples of all nations, baptizing them in the name of the Father and of the Son and of the Holy Spirit…***
>
> Jesus, Matthew 28:19

So this is not a text to prove the need for baptism. It is a call to be immersed into the death of Jesus and then raised to a life lived by faith in Him. It is a call of surrender to God, Jesus, and the Holy Spirit. Baptism is not a work or something we do to be saved. It is not one of a series of checklist steps done to get to be a disciple. It is a life-changing event of love and faith to live by grace and faith. When we share the good news of Jesus, baptism is the natural response.

So do not hurry past the Jesus message so you can focus on baptism. Do not confuse the message with the response to the message. When you do that, you will end baptizing lots of people but making few disciples. Do not assume that people understand the good news and your job is to help them understand the response. Help them understand the message of Jesus, and you will be surprised at how little you need to convince them of the response.

I have spent my life in fellowship with the churches of Christ. They have a strong emphasis on baptism. But often, we were guilty of talking about the response more than the message. So we ended up baptizing over 90 percent of our children as they grew up. And then wondered why only 50 percent or so stayed faithful. Making disciples is more than baptizing people.

Tell the message of Jesus. And make new disciples by baptizing them into the death of Jesus as an act of love for their God. As an act of faith in their Savior. Then teach them to make other followers because they love the people in their world. Let God's love compel them to share God's grace with a world that does know what an amazing gift God has given them. Just like you did with them.

Followers making followers.

WHY **Aren't Followers Making More Followers?**

As disciples of Jesus, we love God with every part of our being.

We love our neighbors as ourselves.

In response to God's grace, we were crucified with Christ and now live a new life.

Every Christian I know would say they are in favor of reaching lost people. Jesus did that, and we want to be like Him. He told us to make more followers, and we want to obey Him.

So why are we not making more and more followers of Jesus?

Is it because we think this is something we should do, but…well, you know…it is someone else's job? Is it that we think we do not know anyone who needs Jesus?

> ***So whoever knows the right thing to do and fails to do it, for him it is sin.***
> James 4:17

You know that making disciples is the right thing to do.

So if you are not…?

Maybe it would help if we took a deeper look into some of the reasons why we might not be living as followers who make followers.

CHAPTER 6

I KNOW I SHOULD, BUT...

I do not think I have ever heard any Christians say they do not want anyone else to find out about Jesus. Every church will embrace the theory that we should be telling the world the good news that Jesus died for their sins. It is the reality of putting that theory into practice that seems so difficult. Most churches simply are not growing. They struggle to make disciples of their own children...much less those outside the church. What growth most churches see is really only troop transfer. You know what that is: members of the Lord's army shifting membership around. The army is not growing. So for every church that grows by having a Christian family join them, there is a church that just got smaller when that family left.

Few churches have a significant number of first-generation Christians. They celebrate the occasional conversion. They pledge to try harder. But the truth is that most churches are much more concerned with themselves than with others. Buildings are built to be used by us. Professionals are hired to minister to us. We have extensive programs to help us grow. And though these things may not be detrimental to growth in and of themselves, they do reveal where our focus lies. Even our language betrays us. Most churches have fully supported ministers, but there are not many evangelists.

I have to admit, however, that by blaming the church collectively for our failure to make disciples, I may be missing the point. The real question is why more individual disciples are not committed to making other disciples. I assume you want to make disciples for Jesus or you would not be reading this book. But just in case...

Let's look at some of the reasons we are not reaching people for Jesus.

Sometimes We Need a Reminder

Love God and love your neighbors. Tell them the story of Jesus. Help them decide to participate in the death and resurrection of Jesus. We are God's ambassadors in this world telling everyone that Jesus died for them. Everyone. But sometimes we need some help to understand what this means.

His name was Cornelius, and he was a good man. He and his family were devout, and they believed in the one God. He was a generous giver to those in need, and he prayed regularly. Most of us would love to have church members that committed. But there was still something missing in the life of Cornelius. He did not know Jesus. However, God was listening to his prayers and sent an angel to assure him his prayers and his giving had come before God. The angel told him to send for Peter.

This amazing story is found in Acts 10 and is a wonderful example of seekers who become followers. Cornelius was a good man who needed Jesus. God connected him to a believer. That is how God works. He hears seekers and connects them to believers. And Peter was a believer. But there was one small problem.

Cornelius Is Not One of Us...

Peter was a good Jew, and Jews did not associate with Gentiles. But as you know, Peter had become a follower of Jesus. He was an evangelist. He was making followers of Jesus. God knew that this might be a difficult—even confusing—assignment for Peter. So He prepared him. While praying on his rooftop one afternoon, Peter became hungry. He fell into a trance, and God showed him a vision. In the vision, there were plenty of animals available, and Peter was told to kill and eat. However, in accordance with Jewish law, Peter refused to eat any unclean animals. God showed him this vision two more times.

While Peter was still wondering about the meaning of his experience, the men sent by Cornelius showed up. The Spirit told Peter to go with them because He had sent them. There it is again—the Holy Spirit connecting seekers and believers. So Peter went. When he arrived, Cornelius had a crowd of family and friends waiting to hear what Peter had to say. Peter acknowledged that as a Jew, he was not to associate with Gentiles, but he also made it clear that God had shown him not to consider any man impure or unclean.

Peter then shared the good news of Jesus: God does not play favorites. He accepts men from any nation who fear Him and do right, and that peace comes through the Lord Jesus. He talked of Jesus being killed and raised from the dead; He will judge the living and the dead; that everyone who believes receives forgiveness of sins through His name.

The story ends with Peter baptizing Cornelius and his friends and family in the name of Jesus Christ. He then stayed with them for a few more days. Peter, a committed follower of Jesus. Cornelius, a seeker who needed Jesus. God connected them by nudging Peter into realizing everyone needs Jesus.

I wonder who in your world is praying right now? Are you the answer to their prayers? Has God nudged you to talk to someone? Is there anyone you have not been willing to talk to about Jesus?

Why are you not telling others about Jesus?

I'd Like to Be a Disciple Maker, But...

There are always ~~excuses~~ reasons why you are not being a disciple maker. So if you have already started forming a list of why you are not making disciples, realize that you are not the first one of God's people to find excuses not to follow the call of God in your life. In fact, one of the great heroes of Scripture did not want to submit to God's call at first either. His name was Moses, and God called him to deliver His people from the bondage of Egypt. In

Exodus 3 and 4, you can read the list of excuses Moses used not to answer that call.

It may be similar to the list of excuses you have when you realize God is calling you to deliver people from the bondage of their sin by becoming a Jesus follower. See if any of these sound familiar.

But I Am Just An Average Member... Nothing Special About Me

Moses asked it this way: "Who am I...?" He had been away from Egypt and God's people for forty years. He was a shepherd with a past he would just as soon forget. Surely there were people more qualified to lead the people out of Egypt. But God called Moses.

In the same way we assume making disciples is the job of the preacher. Or maybe the elders. Or the really mature Christians. Surely God does not expect the average—just a regular member—Christian to be entrusted with something as important as making disciples.

Of course, I do not see where God ever makes distinctions like "average" or "regular" members. If God's plan is for the preachers and elders to reach all the lost people, it is going to take a lot more of them. And they do not know the people in your world. You know the people in your neighborhood and they know you. You know the people where you work, where you go to school; you know the people at the ballfield and at your local restaurant. You have credibility to speak among your friends and family.

When Moses raised this objection, God reminded him that He would be with him. Moses may have seen himself as an ordinary man, but with God at his side, he became an extraordinary leader. So remember what Jesus said, "***I am with you always...***" He does not send us into this world to make disciples by ourselves. He is with us. All the way to the end of this age. It is scary, exhilarating, nerve-racking, exciting, and intimidating to live your life as a disciple maker.

But Jesus is with you. With you when you talk about your faith, with you when you help someone in the name of Jesus, with you when you invite them to worship with your family. He is there.

You are just like Peter and John.

> ***Now when they saw the boldness of Peter and John, and perceived that they were uneducated, common men, they were astonished. And they recognized that they had been with Jesus.***
> Acts 4:13

Common, ordinary Christians doing extraordinary things because we are doing them with Jesus.

What If I Get Asked a Question and Don't Know the Answer?

For Moses, it was a theological question about God's name: *What if they ask me Your name? What do I tell them?* It is still a question I hear today: "What if they ask me a question I cannot answer?" If you aren't careful, it can become a paralyzing fear. You will not talk about Jesus until you are prepared for any question that might be asked. And of course, you are never quite sure you even know all the questions, much less all the answers. So you do nothing.

You will never have all the answers to every question that someone might ask. You probably will not anticipate all the questions either. When Moses tried this excuse, God gave him a basic truth that answers almost every question. *"**I AM WHO I AM**."* God is who He is. That is the fundamental truth on which Moses was to rely: God is.

In the same way, remember the most important thing to know: Jesus. When in doubt, Jesus is the answer. Jesus, who died for our sins, was buried, and was raised on the third day. That is the basic truth on which you rely. That is the foundation for making disciples. Without this core truth, nothing else will matter anyway. You can discuss things, you can get help in answering questions, or you can admit you do not know the answer to every question. But you do have one thing you know for certain: Jesus died for our sins, and God raised him from the dead. How to become a disciple is rooted in this truth. How to live as a disciple is grounded in this truth. Baptism, lifestyle, and communion/community are all grounded in this one truth. So this is the one thing that absolutely has to be communicated. If you know this truth, and if you have made this truth your life, you are ready to talk to friends and family about becoming a disciple of Jesus.

But I Am Not Really Good Enough...

Most of us really would like to help others become followers of Jesus, but we are not really good disciples ourselves. At least, not as good as we should be. We still have sins that trip us up on our walk. We battle secret addictions. There are so many good things that we do not do as well as we should. And this life is hard. Sometimes it is all we can do to try to follow Jesus ourselves—much less teach anyone else.

Moses talked about it from a little different perspective. He worried that the people would not believe him or listen to him. They would say that God had not ever appeared to him. It is the same worry we have. I am not good enough. I know it. God knows it. The people I want to reach for Jesus probably know it.

God answered Moses by giving him signs that He had sent him on this mission: staffs that turned into snakes and hands that became leprous. Proof that God was with him. But we, too, have a sign that God is with us. How we live and what we do for others are the proof that God is with us.

We are not perfect, but we are forgiven. Imagine what we would be without Jesus. And we are being transformed more and more every day into the image of Jesus. We are getting better. In the next few chapters, we will explore what it means to live forgiven and how that is important in making disciples. Then we will talk about serving others and how that service gives credibility to our words about Jesus.

So you do not have to be perfect to teach others to follow Jesus. But you do have to be a follower. If you love God and love others, you are ready to make disciples. If you believe Jesus died for you and that God raised Him from the dead, you know enough. If you have been crucified with Jesus and raised to a new life, you are a follower ready to make other followers. You are good enough because Jesus makes you good enough. After all, we are not making followers in our image, but followers of Jesus. We are inviting others to join us on the journey that leads to forever life.

But It Is Not My Gift...

Moses to God:

"I never have been very good with words. Talking to people just does not come naturally to me. I don't think well on my feet. Never have and never will."

One of my friends talking to me:

"Some people are just natural at telling others about Jesus. You are good at it. You never meet a stranger, you love to talk to people, and you are a natural storyteller. I want lost people to know about Jesus, and I am sure glad we have people like you with that gift. It is just not *my* talent."

God to Moses:

> ***"Who has made man's mouth? Who makes him mute, or deaf, or seeing, or blind? Is it not I, the LORD? Now therefore go, and I will be with your mouth and teach you what you shall speak"***
> Exodus 4:11-12.

Me to my friend:

"Jesus saved us, and we have given our lives to Him. He told us to go into our world and make other followers. And Jesus will be with us when we do this."

God to Moses:

"Is there not Aaron, your brother, the Levite? I know that he can speak well. Behold, he is coming out to meet you, and when he sees you, he will be glad in his heart. You shall speak to him and put the words in his mouth, and I will be with your mouth and with his mouth and will teach you both what to do"
Exodus 4:14-15.

Me to my friend:

"I appreciate the way you are letting God mold you into a faithful Christian. Your friends see that, and I know you are invested in helping other people. Get the conversation started and at some point I will be happy to join in."

I often tell people in my church that I am happy to be the designated "closer" for those times when they come to a point where they want and need help sharing the story of Jesus. But they have to be in the process. They are the connection to the person they hope to make a disciple. They vouch for me. They give me credibility. I even tell them they have to buy the coffee or host the meal.

God told Moses that Aaron would be his partner in delivering their people from slavery. Aaron had a skill set Moses evidently did not have. There are people to partner with you in making disciples.

Live faithful in your world. Serve others in your world. Tell your story. Learn their story. Invite them for meals or to church. Start the conversation. Jesus is right there with you. And when you need help, find those who can help; those with a skill set you do not have. Commit to continue discipling the new follower. Work together.

After all, it is really not a matter of talent. It is a matter of commitment to obeying Jesus.

Okay, Let Me Be Honest. I Am Just Not Going to Do It.
That is basically what Moses told God. He told God to send someone else. Now that is some real life honesty there. I do not know exactly what Moses was thinking. Maybe he just did not want to revisit his past by going into Egypt. Perhaps he really thought that he could not do it—no matter what God said. Or he was too scared. God called Moses, and Moses told Him to get someone else.

Now think for a moment how we talk about reaching lost people for Jesus. We sing songs about seeking the lost; we pray for missionaries and lost people; we nod at the sermons about reaching our neighbors. Some of us have even preached those sermons. We are in favor of making disciples until we go outside the building into our world.

And do nothing.

It's as if we are telling God to get someone else to reach our friends and family with the good news of Jesus. We say we love God and Jesus, but ignore what we were told to do. We claim to love our neighbor as ourselves, but never say a word about the good news that can save them.

Moses had a lot of reasons excuses not to answer God's call. God patiently dealt with each of them. But when Moses told God he did not want to go... that is when God got mad. God's anger burned against Moses. You can read it right there in Exodus 4.

So I wonder how God feels about His people today who will not even make the effort to engage their neighbors about Jesus?

But since you are still reading this, I am going to assume that you are committed to exploring how to live as a Great Commission Christian.

So Be Courageous
Perhaps the best thing you can do is just be more like Ananias. He was a follower living in Damascus when the Lord came to him in a vision to connect him with a seeker. The problem for Ananias

was found in who the seeker was—Saul. Saul: the fanatical Jew who was instrumental in the martyrdom of Stephen. Saul: with authority to arrest and persecute Christians.

But Saul had an encounter with Jesus and was told Ananias would come and tell him what he must do.

Here is what the Lord said to Ananias:

> ***And the Lord said to him, "Rise and go to the street called Straight, and at the house of Judas look for a man of Tarsus named Saul, for behold, he is praying, and he has seen in a vision a man named Ananias come in and lay his hands on him so that he might regain his sight."***
> Acts 9:11-12

> ***But Ananias answered, "Lord, I have heard from many about this man, how much evil he has done to your saints at Jerusalem. And here he has authority from the chief priests to bind all who call on your name."***
> Acts 9:13-14

> ***But the Lord said to him, "Go, for he is a chosen instrument of mine to carry my name before the Gentiles and kings and the children of Israel. For I will show him how much he must suffer for the sake of my name."***
> Acts 9:15-16

God's plan was to connect one of His ambassadors with those whose hearts were seeking Him. It had to be scary for Ananias, who loved God and loved his neighbor. But Saul? How do you love someone like that? A follower making followers in his world. But how did Saul get to be part of his world? Wanting to obey God, but quite aware of the danger.

Ananias went anyway. He restored Saul's sight. He baptized him. And Saul became Paul, the Apostle, the follower who spent his life making other followers.

Do not be afraid. Go into your world. Follow Jesus. Love God. Love your neighbor. Make followers. Then they will make followers, who will make followers, who will make followers.

HOW Do I Go Into My World To Make Followers?

Go and Live Forgiven

So how does one live in this world as a follower making other followers of Jesus?

You start by going among the people in your world and living forgiven. As ambassadors for God, we are carrying the message that Jesus died for everyone so they could be reconciled to God. And our lives are the introduction to that message. We must live our belief. The trendy saying from a few years ago was to "walk the talk." And there is truth in that statement.

Life had been hard for Joan. She remembers going to church as a young girl but does not really remember many details. Mostly it was a matter of going where someone invited her. She believed in Jesus in a general sense, but never knew about dying to self and making that kind of commitment. So when a marriage failed and when a child died, well…she lost whatever small kernel of faith she may have had. The whole Jesus story as she had known it seemed unreal. Even the idea of a God who created us and loved us seemed far-fetched.

But it always nagged at her: What if God is real? So one day she sent an email to a handful of friends and relatives explaining what she wanted. She did not think she believed, but she wanted to hear the Jesus story presented by someone who could explain it from an intellectual basis. One of her cousins, Leigh Ann, responded. She expressed her love for Joan and said she knew someone from her church who loved talking about Jesus and would love to visit. She also explained that she was not sure how intellectual this person was, but that he made it pretty simple to understand.

That is how my wife and I met Joan. God connected seekers and believers. We spent several weeks just visiting with Joan. Hearing her story. Sharing our story. Talking about Jesus stories. One day it all clicked. She understood what it meant to accept by faith that God is real. She understood that Jesus knew everything about her and loved her anyway. She decided to die with Jesus and be raised to new life.

Leigh Ann was there for her baptism. After it was over, she gave Joan a beautiful bracelet with one word on it. *Forgiven.* I think someone had given it, or one like it, to Leigh Ann when she became a Christian.

Forgiven followers who connect with those in their world to make other followers.

Leigh Ann, Steve, and Marsha who loved the God who had loved and forgiven them shared that good news with Joan.

Because...

The way you live your life prepares people to hear the good news of Jesus. You are a living witness to the truth of the Jesus message. Christians live forgiven, and forgiving, in this world. People do notice. Your life and your character give credibility to your message.

Go into your world, and make disciples by living forgiven.

CHAPTER 7

GO LIVE FORGIVEN

If we are going to be sharing the message of Jesus, we have to believe that message. If we are to share the good news that Jesus died for our sins, then our forgiven lives are the evidence that it is real. We do not have to be perfect—which is a good thing since none of us are. But we do have to be different. Jesus has to be transforming us. We are becoming more like Him every day.

People have to know our story. I am a better person today because of Jesus. I am less selfish and more giving. I think more of others and less of myself. The Holy Spirit is working in me to make me...well, more holy. God's Word is training me to be more righteous. We are more like Jesus every day. So are our families.

Our world can be, too.

When Sinners and Jesus Meet

The story does not even appear in some of the earliest texts of the New Testament, but very early, it was inserted and never removed from succeeding copies. It is, therefore, likely a real story from the life of Jesus that everyone knew and accepted. This story from the first part of John 8 is raw and heartbreaking. But our God is a real God who deals with real people in a real world. It is a story of when God's Son meets sinners.

She was a sinner. No one disputed that, not even Jesus. After all, she was caught in the act. She wasn't just suspected of adultery. It was not a case of circumstantial evidence that led her to confess. She was caught in the act. So the religious leaders dragged her before Jesus. Clearly, this was an attempt to put Jesus in an unfavorable light. After all, they did not even bring the other party with her. If Jesus upheld the law and agreed that stoning her was proper, then He would seem harsh and unloving. If He said to show mercy, then He wouldn't have been upholding the law. They thought they had Jesus between a rock and a hard place.

I do not know her name. I do not even know what happened to the man she was with. I do not know why she was committing adultery. Was she in love? Was this a matter of lust? Was it a business transaction?

So what would Jesus do with a sinner? Jesus could condemn her or excuse her. Or He could give her a chance to change her life.

I know that He wrote in the dirt with His finger. I do not know what He wrote. Was He writing Himself a note to remember it was people like all of these for whom He came to die? Was it a note to this woman that He saw her and loved her? Was He listing the names of her accusers and writing their sins beside them?

Then Jesus told them to stone her. As long as the first stone was cast by the one without sin. The oldest were the first to get it. They were all sinners. Every one of them. No compassion. No love. No forgiveness. Just a harsh judgment of a woman they did not even care about except as an object to discredit Jesus before the people. So one at a time they walked away until there was no one left. No one remained to accuse her.

Neither did Jesus. She encountered Jesus at a time when she was experiencing hate and judgment. She found love and forgiveness instead. Then came the chance to change everything.

> ***And Jesus said, "Neither do I condemn you; go, and from now on sin no more.*** John 8:11

Jesus told this woman to go into her world and live forgiven. Stop sinning. Repentance that leads to forgiveness is not revealed by how you feel, but by how you live.

Followers make followers by going into our world and living forgiven.

Even if you are a sinner.

Get Away From Me Jesus, I Am A Sinner

He was just a regular guy cleaning up after having worked the night shift as a professional fisherman. His brother had become a disciple of Jesus and then converted him. While working on his nets, Jesus asked to use his boat to preach to the crowds. So he rowed Jesus out a way from the shore. That is impressive: work all night, gentle waves, and a long sermon. Just staying awake must have been quite the accomplishment. But it was Jesus preaching, so...

When He was through, Jesus told him to put out to deeper water for a catch of fish. I do not know if Jesus was simply doing them a favor or if He was "paying" for renting the boat. But He was going to provide a catch of fish. This is where our fisherman felt the need to let Jesus know something. There were no fish to be caught. This was a professional fisherman, and he had caught nothing all night. Maybe he wanted to protect Jesus from embarrassment. Maybe he was just genuinely baffled that Jesus would say this.

But it was Jesus. So because it was the Lord, he let down the nets.

And caught more fish than ever before. Maybe more than anyone they knew had ever caught. So many fish that the nets starting breaking from the weight of all the fish. So many fish that the boat filled up and they signaled their partners to bring the other boat. So many fish that both the boats started to sink.

Overwhelming, astounding, unheard of power.

And by now you have figured out that our fisherman is Peter, and this story is told in Luke 5 (and also in Matthew and Mark). Peter was the great preacher and apostle, who became so instrumental in bringing thousands to Jesus as he shared the story with large crowds and with small gatherings. Pentecost, a crippled beggar, Cornelius. That Peter. Inspired by the power of Jesus, Peter gave his life to telling others about Jesus.

Except the story really does not go that way. Not at first. Peter's first reaction to this awesome display of power was to fall to his knees and tell Jesus to get away from him. Because he was a sinner. What did the Son of God with power like this want with an uneducated, ordinary fisherman? Peter knew who he was and what he was. He was a follower, but this kind of power and his weakness just didn't go together.

Until Jesus said this...

> ***"Do not be afraid; from now on you will be catching men." And when they had brought their boats to land, they left everything and followed him.***
> Luke 5:10-11

This is a story for us. We are Jesus followers. His power has been shown in our lives as He transforms us into being more and more like Him. Living forgiven. We know we are great sinners. We know God's grace is greater. Jesus does not run from sinners like us. Instead, He calls us to move from our fear. Fear of rejection; fear that you are not good enough; fear of what others may think; fear of saying the wrong thing; fear of meeting that neighbor; fear of inviting that friend to church; fear of sharing your story with a co-worker.

Follow Him because we are going to catch men.

Followers making followers by living forgiven in our world.

Peter Even Wrote About Living Forgiven

First Peter is a letter of encouragement and instruction written by Peter to Christians trying to figure out how to live as strangers in an evil world. Perhaps remembering a life devoted to catching men for Jesus, Peter has a word for us today about living forgiven to make followers.

> ***But you are a chosen race, a royal priesthood, a holy nation, a people for his own possession, that you may proclaim the excellencies of him who called you out of darkness into his marvelous light.*** 1 Peter 2:9

We have been chosen by God to be His people. We are a nation of believers united by our allegiance to God. We are royal priests having a personal relationship with our God. He is the one who called us from darkness into light. He is the one who made it possible for sinners like us to live forgiven. We are His ambassadors.

And we must say so. We are declaring His excellence to our world. We are God-speakers giving Him credit for our lives and our blessings. We talk about Him. We came out of darkness into light, and we declare His praises to those still in darkness. We give God praise; we tell one another of His greatness; and we proclaim His goodness to a lost world.

We credit God for our successes. Not luck or our talents and hard work. We praise God for healings. We give thanks for our daily bread. Jesus is in our hearts and on our lips.

> ***Beloved, I urge you as sojourners and exiles to abstain from the passions of the flesh, which wage war against your soul. Keep your conduct among the Gentiles honorable, so that when they speak against you as evildoers, they may see your good deeds and glorify God on the day of visitation.***
> 1 Peter 2:11-12

As forgiven people of God, we live differently. We fight against the evil that would come back into our lives. We guard against temptation. We help one another on our spiritual journey. We are not perfect, but we are getting better. Sometimes we do things we should not. But here is what makes Christians different. When we sin, we do not think it is acceptable. We are sorry; we work to correct it; we guard against its happening again.

Our conduct is honorable before the people in our world. Even if they say bad things about us. They did in Peter's day. Christians were called cannibals (lots of talk about eating flesh and drinking blood). Some accused them of incest (lots of talk about brothers, sisters, and love). Today, it is that we are unloving or judgmental.

But when they see how we live, and the good deeds we do, they get a glimpse of God. Some of them may even be led to recognize and seek God. Living as forgiven people points to the God who makes it possible.

Giving Us an Opportunity to Make More Followers

> ***Likewise, wives, be subject to your own husbands, so that even if some do not obey the word, they may be won without a word by the conduct of their wives***
> 1 Peter 3:1

The power of living forgiven. Sometimes our actions really do speak louder than our words. The way we live gives credibility to our message. Our lives are a reflection of the message. Live forgiven, and give God the glory. People are listening. And they certainly are watching.

> ***but in your hearts honor Christ the Lord as holy, always being prepared to make a defense to anyone who asks you for a reason for the hope that is in you; yet do it with gentleness and respect,...***
> 1 Peter 3:15

We obey the greatest commandment by loving God and His Son with everything we have. Jesus sits on the throne of our heart. So we live forgiven and speak of God's glory, which makes some of the people in our world curious. They may even want to know how and why we live the way we do. After all, living forgiven does lead to a different lifestyle than the people around us, so they might ask us why, and we must be ready to answer them.

Living forgiven opens doors of opportunity to talk about Jesus.

"But why won't you fudge on your expense account?"

"Why do you get up every Sunday and go to church?"

"You mean you are going to forgive your wife and try to work it out?"

"I heard you got bad news from the doctor."

And on and on it goes. We are different, and that difference sparks conversation.

Be ready to give your Jesus answer.

But when you do, remember the second greatest command. Love your neighbor. Do not talk down to them. Do not lecture. Do not be defensive. Do not argue.

Be gentle. Be respectful.

You are representing Jesus. You are giving them a glimpse into how Jesus people live. You are an ambassador brought from darkness into light.

You are living forgiven, and people notice.

CHAPTER 8

HOW LIVING FORGIVEN LOOKS

God forgives sinners and then uses them to bring other sinners back to Him. But what does it really look like to live forgiven?

His story is one of the most well-known in the Bible. Even as a youth, he had great courage and confidence in God. After all, when he was just a young shepherd boy, he killed the Philistine giant, Goliath. He was one of the greatest kings of Israel and in the New Testament, he is referred to as a man after God's own heart.

However, he also committed adultery with the wife of one of his commanders, lied about it, had the husband killed, and then took the woman to be his wife. The story of David and Bathsheba is recorded in 2 Samuel 11 and 12. Nathan, a prophet of God, confronted David about his sin. David did not make excuses, he did not blame Bathsheba, and he did not take it out on Nathan.

> ***David said to Nathan, "I have sinned against the Lord." And Nathan said to David, "The Lord also has put away your sin; you shall not die.***
> 2 Samuel 12:13

David was forgiven, but what did that mean for how he was going to live in the future and what does it mean for how he talked about God?

David himself actually wrote about how he was going to live forgiven. You can read his thoughts about it in one of his psalms.

Psalm 51: Living Forgiven

This is a look into the heart of David. It is a blueprint for how forgiven sinners make followers of Jesus.

Ask for Forgiveness.

1 Have mercy on me, O God,
according to your steadfast love;
according to your abundant mercy
blot out my transgressions.
2 Wash me thoroughly from my iniquity,
and cleanse me from my sin!

9 Hide your face from my sins,
and blot out all my iniquities.

Confess Your Sin.

3 For I know my transgressions,
and my sin is ever before me.

4 Against you, you only, have I sinned
and done what is evil in your sight,
so that you may be justified in your words
and blameless in your judgment.

17 The sacrifices of God are a broken spirit;
a broken and contrite heart, O God, you will not despise.

Be Healed.

7 Purge me with hyssop, and I shall be clean;
wash me, and I shall be whiter than snow.
8 Let me hear joy and gladness;
let the bones that you have broken rejoice.

Be Restored.

10 Create in me a clean heart, O God,
and renew a right spirit within me.
11 Cast me not away from your presence,
and take not your Holy Spirit from me.
12 Restore to me the joy of your salvation,
and uphold me with a willing spirit.

Make Followers.

13 Then I will teach transgressors your ways,
and sinners will return to you.
14 Deliver me from bloodguiltiness, O God,
O God of my salvation,
and my tongue will sing aloud of your righteousness.

15 O Lord, open my lips,
and my mouth will declare your praise.

This Is Exactly What Ken Did

Ken became a follower of Jesus as a young teenager. He married his childhood sweetheart. The marriage survived mostly because of his wife, but the following Jesus did not. At least it did not for a long time. Ken ran with gangs, bootlegged liquor into dry counties, and lived the kind of life you would associate with those activities. But his wife stayed faithful to the Lord, and God kept working on Ken. In his later years, Ken came back to the Lord. And he started making up for lost time. Sat right down near the front, worshiped with enthusiasm, and started telling others about Jesus. In fact, his row at church was filled with people he had brought to Jesus.

Ken had a dream. He wanted to reach his fellow alcoholics with the good news of Jesus. He wanted to reach people who had given up on church. Or at least thought church had given up on them. People who did not believe Jesus would want them. People like...well, like Ken used to be.

So he wanted to start doing church in a bar. Church in a bar. He did not have any grand plan or agenda. Ken's dream was to take the gospel into a place where people who needed Jesus felt comfortable. I happened to be in one of the first meetings where Ken shared his vision. I loved it. Loved his passion. Loved the idea of a guy like Ken being an evangelist. At a church that would meet in a bar. But seriously, how was he going to find a bar that would let a church meet there? Ken started praying. Started talking about his dream. And within weeks, he found a place. A bar that would let a church service be held on a Sunday morning.

A sinner now living forgiven. A follower who wanted to reach other followers. And God blessed the vision. People started coming: some who had messed up their lives and were ashamed to go into a church building; some who had trouble staying sober enough to show up at a regular church; some who were cynical; some who were searching.

Ken's kind of people. Ken believed that Jesus died for each one of them. So he shared his story. And he shared God's story in Jesus. He started making more followers. More and more people got interested in that story. So God raised up other followers to make followers. A football coach and his school teacher wife. A plumber. A track coach.

Followers making followers. Telling the Jesus story. Sharing their story. Inviting others into the Jesus life. Baptizing sinners in swimming pools and horse tanks. Followers living forgiven. Radically committed to making other followers. So every month God adds another three or four to His kingdom who start living forgiven, who bring their friends to hear the good news, who become followers.

Live Forgiven and Model Forgiveness

We have already looked at the kind of follower that Philip was in Chapter Two. He was a follower who made other followers. He shared the good news of Jesus in Jerusalem, in Samaria, and with a government official from Ethiopia. He was one of those special servants in Acts 6 who helped alleviate a potential crisis involving care of the widows in the early church. One of the other special servants was Stephen. The same Stephen who was killed by the Jewish High Priest and his followers. They were Jews so committed to the way things were that they refused to listen to the truth of Jesus. Stephen presented Jesus in such a powerful way that they killed him, which led to Philip and many other believers having to flee Jerusalem. After his encounter with the Ethiopian, Philip eventually ended up in Caesarea where he continued to follow Jesus and to evangelize others. And I wonder if every time Philip talked about Jesus he remembered his friend and preaching buddy, Stephen.

Meanwhile...a man named Saul was doing everything he could to destroy what he believed to be a false religion. He was the one instrumental in the stoning of Stephen. He went from town to town, seeking out followers of Jesus and throwing them into jail.

Until Saul encountered Jesus. Until a courageous follower named Ananias refused to make excuses and went to help Saul become a follower. Until Ananias baptized him. Until God commissioned him to take the gospel all over the Gentile world. Until his name was changed from Saul to Paul. Maybe Paul thought about Stephen every time he preached, too, though for different reasons.

Saul/Paul and Philip Meet

It was on one of Paul's missionary journeys when it happened. He and his team had traveled from Tyre through Ptolemais.

> ***On the next day we departed and came to Caesarea, and we entered the house of Philip the evangelist, who was one of the seven, and stayed with him.***
> Acts 21:8

I wonder what Paul thought when someone suggested they stay at Philip's house. For that matter...what did Philip think when he heard Paul was in town? The man who murdered his friend was coming to stay in his home. Paul must have wondered how he would be received by a man who certainly remembered the darkest days of Paul's life before he became of follower of Jesus.

Here is what I imagine must have happened. Paul knocks on the door and Philip answers.

"Philip, my name is Paul, but you probably remember me as Saul, and I am so, so sorry for..."

And I believe Philip stopped him right there.

"I remember, but you are forgiven. I have heard of your conversion and that you are telling others of God's grace. I forgive you. You are now my brother. Welcome to my home."

And I suspect he hugged him. I think tears flowed down both their cheeks. Paul was a living witness to the story of Jesus. His life was a testimony to God's grace and forgiveness. So was the life of Philip. God's mercy and grace change us. The world notices. But we also extend forgiveness to others.

So we live forgiven by...

Accepting God's forgiveness and living new lives free from sin.

By confessing our sins when we do not live like Jesus.

Being healed and restored and extending that grace to others.

Speaking the praises of the God who sent His Son to save us.

And by making other followers who will live forgiven in their world.

WHERE **Do I Go In My World To Make Followers?**

Go Where People Need To Be Served

What does it mean to "go into all the world"? It means to engage with the people in your neighborhood, and the people with whom you work or go to school, and the people among your friends and family. Your world is made up of the people around you who have needs you can meet. People who need food and shelter, people who are lonely, people who are living lives devoid of purpose, hope, and joy. People you serve. And that service plants seeds in hearts. Seeds about the good news of Jesus.

Jesus said it this way.

> ***In the same way, let your light shine before others, so that they may see your good works and give glory to your Father who is in heaven.***
> Matthew 5:16

Just like Peter and John in the temple courts, we serve people in the name of Jesus. We serve them so they can see God. Serving people in the name of Jesus gives credibility to our message.

We live forgiven so that the people in our world will know that Jesus changes lives. Our lives are our testimony.

We serve so the people in our world will be pointed to Jesus. Our service becomes our witness.

So how do I serve as a follower to make other followers?

CHAPTER 9

LIVE TO SERVE

Let's be honest. It is hard to love my neighbor as myself. I know Jesus said that is the second most important command—right behind loving God. But who really is my neighbor? Is it the people who live close to me? What about people with whom I work or attend school? Are friends also neighbors? Is it everybody I know? What about people I do not know? And what does it mean to love them? How do I love someone as much as I love myself? These questions have been asked for generations. In fact, when Jesus gave these commands in Luke 10, an expert in religious law asked Him to define the idea of "your neighbor." Exactly who is my neighbor?

The man was actually looking to justify the way he had been living. Maybe even justify the way he wanted to live. Just who is it he has to love? Who is it we have to love as we love ourselves?

Jesus answered by telling a story. It is one of the most famous lessons He ever taught. It is most often called the story of the Good Samaritan.

So What Exactly Am I Supposed To Learn?

Jesus told this story so we would understand who our neighbor is and what it means to love them as ourselves.

So...

My neighbor is anyone in my world who has a need. The Samaritan saw a man in need of care. Other people had looked at him but did not see him. Instead of loving him, they went out of their way to go around him. See the people in your world.

They have needs you can meet. It may be as simple as taking over a meal when someone is sick. Or mowing a yard or pet sitting while they are out of town or unloading furniture.

Notice the person at work who never gets invited to lunch. Or the classmate who sits by himself. Or a single mom overwhelmed with work, kids, and life. How about the guy sitting on the curb every morning when you go to work? Needs can be physical or emotional. The may be temporary or ongoing. The point is your world is full of people who have needs. See the person...and see the need.

The Good Samaritan felt compassion for this wounded person. You would think that the religious leaders who passed him by would have felt that way. I don't know if they were on their way to an important meeting and were so preoccupied that they did not even think twice about this man. Maybe they assumed that the mess he was in was his fault so that in some way freed them from any obligation to help.

People need help for all sorts of reasons. Life is hard. But to determine someone's worthiness to be helped is missing the point of being a follower of Jesus. If anyone understands what it means to have someone else bear the consequences of bad choices, it is a Jesus follower. If anyone understands that life is not fair, it is the person who knows Jesus died for sins that were not His own.

The point is that, for whatever reason, people need help. Tears, hunger, pain, loneliness, and despair are real. People hurt. See them, recognize the need, and then do something about it.

The Samaritan ministered to the wounded man. He took care of his wounds and took him to a place he could recover. So fix a meal. Even better, invite them to eat it with you. Babysit for the single mom. Go visit the hospital. Provide a ride to a job interview. Mow the yard. Remember that love acts.

Pay the price to serve. It costs something to help people. Walking while a wounded man sits on your donkey. Putting the cost of recovery on your bill. It may be time...or money...

or energy. It may be uncomfortable. It may be long-term. The Samaritan was up to his elbows in blood and dirt.

Go into your world, and love your neighbor as yourself.

Because Jesus told you to be like this Samaritan.

I Know This Because of My Wife

We were working in the front yard when it happened. My wife was mowing and I was using the weed eater. But really I was spending a lot of time looking at my neighbor's yard. It was pretty grown up. They had moved in a couple of months before, and we had only talked to them a few times. I was pretty sure our new neighbor was a single mom, and it was just her and her teenage daughter. Then I noticed something. My wife had run the lawn mower across our driveway and into their yard. At first, I decided she must have had a stroke and lost control of the mower. Except that she did seem to know what she was doing. She was mowing their yard.

It was right about then that our neighbor, Kathy, pulled in her driveway. We shut everything off, and I watched as Kathy got out of her car and asked my wife, Marsha, what she was doing. Marsha just told her that today was our day for yard work, and it looked like she could use some help. So Marsha was going to mow her front and that I was going to weed eat, edge, and then mow the back.

As we visited, two facts came out. Kathy had never learned to mow a yard. Her ex-husband had always done it. The second fact was that Marsha got to tell her we were doing it because of Jesus. He had been good to us, so we tried to be good to others. Over the next few weeks, Kathy bought a lawn mower, learned to mow (Marsha had told her I'd be glad to show her) and now keeps up her yard herself. Even mows the strip between our houses.

See needs. Feel their pain. Don't judge.

Do something about it, even if it costs you something.

In the name of Jesus.

And Someday This Happens...

Hitchhiking is a major form of transportation in Cuba. Poor roads and few cars make traveling difficult. If you own a vehicle, it is your civic responsibility to fill your car with hitchhikers, dropping them off at the major intersections near their destination.

They were an older couple not that different from all the others hoping to catch a ride. He was one of the few farmers in Cuba still working family land, and they were trying to get a ride home.

Tony Fernandez had a vehicle. It was not in very good shape, but it still ran. It might not even be street legal in many parts of the world, but Tony and his friends kept it running. Tony is a preacher in the city of Matanzas, and he works for Herald of Truth coordinating radio responses and planting churches across the island.

Tony offered the farmer and his wife a ride. While they traveled, he learned parts of their story. Two of their sons had died, one by suicide. Life had not been easy or kind to them. When they got to the turn-off by their farm, Tony did not stop. He was taking them all the way home. They protested. It was too far and the road was too rough, but to Tony that did not matter. They had a need, and he believed in helping. He prayed with them. He listened. He cared.

He asked them if they would like to hear more about life with Jesus. They did. Tony later baptized them both. They told their remaining son and his wife about Jesus. They, too, were baptized. Now there is a house church that meets at the farm.

Tony is a follower of Jesus. He was out and about in his world. He was living as a believer. And when he encountered this couple, he did what believers do. He served them in the name of Jesus. He shared the good news of Jesus. And they become followers. Then they made followers of their son and his wife. Now their house church is actively involved in making more followers.

Because Tony went into his world with the intention of making other followers. Because God connected him with a couple who needed Jesus.

Because Tony told the story.

Go into your world.

People in need are waiting.

CHAPTER 10

IN THE NAME OF JESUS

As followers of Jesus, we are going to do what He did. That's what followers do. He fed, healed, and was a friend to the people He encountered in His ministry. So we will minister to and serve others in the same way.

Jesus told us to love our neighbors and illustrated exactly what that meant in the story of the Good Samaritan. You take care of people you encounter in your life. Disciples obey what Jesus told us to do.

We serve others because Jesus did. But that service opens doors. Living forgiven gives us authenticity and serving in the name of Jesus gives us credibility as we seek to be followers who make followers.

It works like this.

Do You Need Some Help?

It started in a shopping center parking lot. Two women were struggling with their purchases and clearly intending to walk home with their bags. Pat saw them—and I need to tell you here that Pat is retired, a widow, and a Jesus follower—and wondered if they needed help. She gave them a ride back to where they were living. Though their English was poor, they were appreciative, and Pat was able to find out they were Bhutanese refugees from Nepal.

They needed help learning how to live in a culture that was as different as night and day from the tents in which they had lived in Nepal. So Pat offered to help. Then she found out they had lots and lots of friends. So Pat recruited a few people from her church family to help her love on these neighbors. They helped them learn to shop, speak English, find jobs, learn to drive, learn to cook, and enroll their children in school.

Pat and her fellow believers also invited them to come to church, which led to a Bible class, then an additional class for the teens, and then more teachers for the children's classes. Eventually a van was needed to transport our Bhutanese friends to church. Then Pat's church rented an apartment in the complex where many of the refugees lived so Bible studies could be held there.

It took an enormous investment of time, money, and resources. It took lots of followers of Jesus giving furniture, time, and extra money to help. Pat found neighbors in her world by seeing them in a parking lot, realizing they needed help, and then providing it.

Pat also loved God enough to be sure and let her new friends know why she was helping and why so many of her friends from church were willing to help. That was over five years ago, and we have literally lost count of the many Bhutanese who have become followers of the Jesus that most of them had never heard of before.

Because Pat is a follower of Jesus who loves God and her neighbors.

Remembering the Main Thing

Serving other people is really about Jesus. It is not actually about us or the people we serve. Loving others and serving them is rooted in the greatest command: Love God with everything we have. Sometimes it is even possible to forget why we are so busy with other people.

Martha was hosting a dinner in her home in honor of Jesus. Her sister, Mary, and her brother, Lazarus, were also there. This was the same Lazarus whom Jesus had raised from the dead some time before. The sisters were dedicated followers of Jesus, but Martha had a lot going on. It is no small matter to host the Son of God in your home. There were guests to seat, a house to get ready, and a meal to prepare. Martha was distracted, overwhelmed, and frustrated.

And where was her sister? Sitting at the feet of Jesus listening to Him teach. It obviously irritated Martha because she approached Jesus about it.

> ***And she went up to him and said, "Lord, do you not care that my sister has left me to serve alone? Tell her then to help me."***
> Luke 10:40

Martha was so out of sorts that she had forgotten why she was serving in the first place. There she was, taking out her frustration on Jesus Himself, telling Him to get Mary up to help. She was so busy doing things *for* Jesus that she forgot she was doing *because* of Jesus.

It is an easy thing to do. Helping people can be exhausting and draining. It can seem like you are the only one who cares or is even trying to serve. It can be frustrating when everyone does not jump in to help in the area of need that you so clearly see and are working in. But when you start focusing on the people who are not serving, you are in danger of missing the point.

Jesus pointed this out to Martha.

> ***But the Lord answered her, "Martha, Martha, you are anxious and troubled about many things, but one thing is necessary. Mary has chosen the good portion, which will not be taken away from her."***
> Luke 10:41-42

Service is an act of love, not a duty. Do not let serving others become a burden or a chore. Only one thing matters: Jesus. When you forget that, then serving others becomes a stressful, frustrating job.

The one thing is Jesus. Do not let helping people distract you so that you lose your focus. When you become worried and upset about helping people, it is hard to remember that you love them.

And do not worry about what others are doing or not doing. Do not try to make others serve like you do.

Love God. Love others.
Go into your world, and help those in need.
Because of Jesus.

Serving and Sharing Jesus Go Together

And he went throughout all Galilee, teaching in their synagogues and proclaiming the gospel of the kingdom and healing every disease and every affliction among the people.
Matthew 4:23

If you want to follow Jesus by doing what He did, you will be involved in serving and sharing. I grew up in a church environment where there was great emphasis placed on teaching people about Jesus. I did not hear the same kind of importance placed on serving people. I do want to acknowledge that I saw a great deal of service done in the name of Jesus, but it was more an individual thing, not something I remember the church doing. The youth activities I remember where mostly door knocking to try and talk about Jesus or they were service projects. But the service projects were for our members.

There is nothing wrong with either of these, of course. We should talk about Jesus, and we should take care of our spiritual family. But I remember few church activities that were designed for community service. That was perhaps an imbalance that needed to be corrected. And, at least in the church circles I am in now, we did correct it.

There are many projects and programs to serve our community. Reading in "adopted" schools, stocking food pantries and clothing rooms to share with the local community, building houses, digging water wells. These are all good things that we should do. But I hear little anymore about telling the good news of the kingdom. Oddly and unfortunately, it is possible to go on numerous youth mission trips and never say a word about Jesus or your faith.

Jesus healed people because they had needs, and He loved them. But He also addressed their greatest need. And that need was to know the good news that God sent Jesus so they could live with God forever.

Jesus was clear about this to His disciples.

And he called the twelve together and gave them power and authority over all demons and to cure diseases, and he sent them out to proclaim the kingdom of God and to heal.
Luke 9:1-2

Jesus told His disciples to heal and tell. Deal with the physical needs of people and tell them of the kingdom of God. Sharing the good news of the kingdom is done with hands of service and lips of praise.

And the disciples did what He said.

And they departed and went through the villages, preaching the gospel and healing everywhere.
Luke 9:6

There are hurting people all around you. They're in your neighborhood, in your schools, in your family, at the ballpark, in your coffee shop, and well...everywhere you do life. You can help them. See them, hear them, help them. But most of those people do not know Jesus. They are not followers. They are lost, and you can help them. Pray for them, invite them to a meal, share your Jesus story, tell stories from your community of faith, invite them to church, ask if you can share a story with them.

Because that is what Jesus did.

When the crowds learned it, they followed him, and he welcomed them and spoke to them of the kingdom of God and cured those who had need of healing.
Luke 9:11

Jesus told His disciples what to do, but He also showed them what to do. There is a lesson here for leaders. If you want to lead a church that is active in seeking and saving the lost, you must lead by example. Jesus did.

As a follower of Jesus, you want to do what He did. Serve and tell.

Both/And, Not Either/Or

It is difficult for people to hear your message if your actions—or more accurately, your inaction—get in the way. Do not be the person who decides to share Jesus with the single mom next door and does it like this...

Walk through the overgrown yard, step around the dirty clothes, ignore the dirty dishes and the dirty baby. Realize the young mom is sick. Not wanting to be insensitive, you do not ask to share the good news right then, so you say something like this.

"I hope you get to feeling better soon. I know Jesus can help you. I'd love to talk to you about it. I'll come back when you are feeling better."

Obviously, that is an exaggeration. Or at least I hope it is. But the truth is that what that young mom needs is her yard mowed, dishes washed, help with childcare, someone to take her to the doctor, and maybe even some help with job skills. Do what she needs. She might want to know why you would help her, so you tell her that you are a Christian. God has been good to you and expects you to be good to others. And if you serve her in those ways, you might find out that she is not just receptive to hearing about Jesus...but even eager.

But at the same time, do not be this person...

You are committed to being like Jesus and loving your neighbor so you get the youth group to mow her yard, you help her enroll in a life skills course your church offers, and you even wash her dishes. You get several of your church friends to chip in and pay for a doctor visit and arrange childcare. Just like Jesus would do.

But what if she is too shy to ask why you would want to help her? You neglect to mention why you are doing all this, so she ends up thinking you and your friends are wonderful people, but nothing really changes. Not permanently. She may get a better job and learn better life skills, but still not see how to live a life of purpose, hope, or joy.

You will have done kingdom business without letting her know she, too, could be part of the kingdom of God.

Or you do mention that you are doing this because of Jesus, but never share more than that; then you have left her worse off in some ways. She will have seen a glimpse of something better than what she has. She will have witnessed community, life with purpose, people of joy, people involved in something bigger than themselves, and she will see people who are making a difference in the world—especially in her world.

She may not even really know who Jesus is. You may leave her admiring this Jesus community but never even knowing that she could be a part of it. There is a time to serve and a time to speak. But speaking without service sure makes it difficult to be heard. Serving without speaking does nothing to help fill the greatest need people have—to know Jesus.

Living forgiven gives authenticity to the message.

Serving in the name of Jesus gives credibility to the message.

But we have to share the message.

WHAT
Do I Do In My World?

Speak Boldly the Good News

When you live forgiven in your world, and when you serve others in your world, you are able to share authentically the good news of Jesus. Just as He does in your life, Jesus offers hope, purpose, and joy to all those in your world. He is the gift of God to forgive sins.

But you do have to tell the story of Jesus.

Just like followers of Jesus have always done.

> ***And every day, in the temple and from house to house, they did not cease teaching and preaching that the Christ is Jesus.***
> Acts 5:42

They never *stopped* doing what some of us have never *started* doing. The early Christians talked about Jesus every day. They talked in private settings with individuals and small groups in homes. They talked publicly to assembled crowds. But they never stopped.

They shared with everyone they could—and in any place they could.

And the message was Jesus.

We go into our world to speak boldly the message of reconciliation found in Jesus.

CHAPTER 11

SPEAK BECAUSE YOU LOVE JESUS

Because you love God and His Son, Jesus, and because you love the people in your world, you will be intentional about making other followers. Jesus saved you, and how you live as a forgiven follower is a witness to God's grace. Because you love God, your service reflects His glory, and because you love others you will let them know that the good news that changed your life is also available to them. You will declare the praises of God because He has brought you from darkness to light. You will tell what God has done for you.

Just like this man.

This Is My Story

He was a mess. I don't know any other way to say it. Lonely, a social outcast, and bullied by the people in his village. He would cry in the night and—perhaps just to feel something—he would cut himself with sharp stones. His demons were so numerous that he called himself "Legion." His was a life with no hope, no joy, no peace, and no purpose.

Until he met Jesus. Legion certainly knew who Jesus was, but now there they were face-to-face. What could Jesus possibly want with a man like him? And there Jesus was calling on the demons to be cast out from this broken man. Legion's first reaction was to beg Jesus not to torture him. Torture? Jesus? I know many think of some kind of physical punishment here, but I wonder if Legion is begging not to tortured by empty promises.

Maybe he was asking for Jesus not to get his hopes up, not to raise false expectations, or to not give him a glimpse of life that he could never really obtain. Just like those in our world who think the whole idea of Jesus is too good to be true. That Jesus can't really change lives. That He cannot deliver on the promise of new life.

Jesus asked what his name was. He wanted to know him. Him…not just the demons that had ruined his life. Jesus was telling him that He knew all about him, yet still wanted to know him. Jesus showing us how to love our neighbor because of how much we love our Father.

You know how the story ends. Legion is healed, the demons are cast out, and he is restored to his right mind. The people in the town rush out to see what has happened and what they see frightens them. Jesus has made a new man out of Legion. Jesus really is stronger than the demons in our lives.

So the people of the town asked Jesus to leave. He was upsetting everything. Nothing would ever be the same if He stayed. Of course not. That is the point. And evidently, that was exactly not what the people of the town wanted. They liked things the way they were.

So Jesus left. He would not stay where He was not wanted. Legion tried to go with Him, but Jesus stopped him. Legion was ready to go wherever Jesus was going. He wanted to be part of the mission of bringing people back to God.

He did get to do that, just not in the way he thought.

> ***And he did not permit him but said to him, "Go home to your friends and tell them how much the Lord has done for you, and how he has had mercy on you."***
> Mark 5:19

Jesus told Legion to go into his world and tell them his story.

That is still what He expects of us today. To go among our friends and family—our world—and tell them what God has done for us. Sharing our story.

I Can Do What He Did

There is incredible power in sharing what Jesus has done in your life. Just ask Todd, Christian, Luke, Chris, or Joe. Todd is an elder at a large church in Texas. He prays for God to send people into his life who do not know Jesus. And God does. One of those people was Christian, a refugee from the Ivory Coast. Todd got to know Christian when he hired him to work in the nursery he managed. Todd and his family basically adopted Christian, helping him learn to function in a culture different than he had ever known. They invited him to family functions and started bringing him to church. He saw up close what a forgiven life looks like. Todd eventually shared the story of Jesus with Christian and ended up baptizing him into Christ.

I love that story so much that I tell it all over the world. I even included it in my book, *Can I Tell You a Story?*

Luke is a young farmer who attends a small church in Idaho. He had a copy of the book and read the story of Todd and Christian. He became convicted that he should be praying the same prayer Todd did. He happened to need another worker for the family farming business. So Luke began to pray for God to bring him someone with whom he could share Jesus.

Enter Chris. Chris was a fairly new Christian himself, but active in sharing his faith. He had a friend named Joe who was recently released from prison. It was at a church fellowship meal that Luke asked if anyone knew someone he could hire. Chris mentioned Joe. Luke hired him, helped find a place for him to live, and helped with transportation. Joe was seeing what it looks like when people live forgiven. Chris and Luke were serving him.

You can guess what happened next. Sharing life together, invitations to come to church, Bible studies. And Joe became a Christian. Because Todd and Christian shared their story, because Chris wanted to help a friend, and because Luke wanted someone with whom he could share Jesus.

And God connected these five men through the power of His Son, Jesus.

Living, serving, sharing the story.

And followers making followers.

Songs from Forgiven Hearts

My wife's mother was on her deathbed. We all knew it, and so did she. But every time we were with her, she wanted to sing. There was one special song she wanted to sing together: *This Is the Day*. It is a song about living in the day the Lord has made and living it rejoicing. It has been somewhat of a family anthem for us. My son's family sings it around the breakfast table every morning, and my daughter's kids sing it with my wife when she takes them to school every morning. So it was special when our whole family would sing around Granny's bed. You could see her trying to sing along with us. We sang it around her grave, too.

Why do Christians sing so much? Because that is what happy people do. My mother-in-law knew death was the beginning of life. She had been a Christian a long time and knew she was forgiven. She knew who she belonged to and where she was going.

Just Like These Christians

It had to be the one of the worst nights ever for Paul and Silas. Imprisoned because they had shared their faith in Jesus and—more specifically—because they freed a slave girl from her demons. That act deprived her owners of the chance to keep making money off of her. The owners of this slave girl then managed to get the townspeople so worked up that the local magistrates had to do something...so they had Paul and Silas beaten and thrown in jail. Where they were singing and praying. Wait...what?

Surely they were depressed, scared, and aware they were in danger of dying in that jail cell. Maybe they were praying for deliverance. Or singing songs of lament.

But what if they were singing songs of praise? They were

followers living forgiven lives. They loved God with everything they had. Surely they sang songs of praise when things were good, and I am just as certain that they sang songs of praise when things were not good.

Just like we do. When we love God, we praise Him. We sing His praises when things are good—and we sing His praises when they are bad. That is our witness and our testimony. We love the God who gave His Son for us so we could have new life. And no matter what happens in that new life, we will praise Him.

Maybe Paul and Silas were praying for deliverance. Or maybe they were praying for strength and courage to face whatever lay before them. Perhaps they were praying for the prisoners around them. Perhaps even praying for the prison warden.

It Was His Worst Nightmare

I imagine he heard them singing and praying. And the chief warden of this prison certainly knew the charges against these Jesus preachers. He had done his job just as he was supposed to do it. There would be no way these two could escape. He had placed Paul and Silas in maximum security and even secured their feet in stocks with chains.

Then something completely out of his control ruined everything. An earthquake struck. The damage occurred right there...in his prison. It rocked the prison to its very foundation. The cell doors were opened and even the chains holding the prisoners broke apart.

Life as this warden knew it was now over. You do not recover from a disaster like this. It did not matter if it was his fault or not. He was told to secure the prisoners, and now they would just walk right out the door. Disgrace would follow. Certainly he would lose his job. Perhaps he would be imprisoned. He might even face death because of this.

Except that no one escaped. The prisoners stayed. All of them. Why would they do that? Surely the earthquake was God's way of delivering Paul and Silas from prison. Why would they even think of how this could affect the jailer? But Paul and Silas were followers of Jesus, singing and praying because they loved God and were living forgiven. And giving this jailer what he needed because they loved their neighbor as themselves. They did for him what he needed and could not do for himself. They stayed.

And Then They Shared the Good News of Jesus

> ***And the jailer called for lights and rushed in, and trembling with fear he fell down before Paul and Silas. Then he brought them out and said, "Sirs, what must I do to be saved?" And they said, "Believe in the Lord Jesus, and you will be saved, you and your household." And they spoke the word of the Lord to him and to all who were in his house. And he took them the same hour of the night and washed their wounds; and he was baptized at once, he and all his family. Then he brought them up into his house and set food before them. And he rejoiced along with his entire household that he had believed in God.***
>
> Acts 16:29-34

There was something clearly different about Paul and Silas, and they obviously cared about their warden. When he saw their lives and realized what they had done for him, he just wanted to know one thing: What did he need to do to be saved? And of course, the one thing was Jesus. Believe in Jesus they told him. It always starts with Jesus. Then they spoke the word of the Lord to him and the others in his household.

The jailer was convicted by their lives, their service, and the story. He washed the wounds left by the beating they had endured. Then he and all his family were baptized. It was then that the celebration started. He served them a meal in his home, and he was filled with joy. All because he decided that he believed. He had become a follower of Jesus.

And all of this happened because he was part of the world

where Paul and Silas lived. God connected him with these believers who were living the forgiven life. They took care of the jailer in his time of crisis. And then they told him the story of Jesus.

Live and serve in the name of Jesus.

And when you get the opportunity... speak boldly.

CHAPTER 12

SPEAK BOLDLY

It started with an invitation to go on a youth group church trip: just one girl asking her friend if she would like to go with her and her church friends to visit a Christian college for High School Day. I never did find out what prompted the invitation, but I do know it was not part of some clever scheme to convert someone. It was just a friend who shared things that were important to her. Her youth group and Jesus were important, so she invited Deanne to go on a trip.

Then she invited her to go to church with her, and Deanne did. Friends sharing things that mattered. As the Youth Minister, I thought visitors ought to have the opportunity to find out why we are the way we are, so...I asked Deanne if she would like to know more about what we believed. And she did. Not because of me, but because she liked our group, she enjoyed the things we did, and she was interested in Jesus. It was not long until Deanne was baptized and set about learning to live as a disciple.

She shared what was going on in her life with her little sister, Denise. She was interested, too. She started coming with her big sister, and she, too, became a disciple. So did their mom. And then their dad. The girls eventually married a couple of Jesus followers from church. Deanne and Charley. Denise and Tim. These two couples even ended up doing ministry together at the same church for decades.

They have had an amazing impact on our world for the kingdom of God. Making disciples, teaching, equipping, and motivating others to follow Jesus with them. The total number of lives impacted by these couples will not be known until eternity.

All because a teenage girl who followed Jesus helped make a disciple of her friend...who helped make a disciple of her sister... then her parents...and on and on it went. And it still does—almost forty years later.

Working with God to be Great Commission disciples making other disciples—followers making followers.

Just Tell Your Story

She had quite a story. Her life had not turned out the way she must have envisioned it when she was a young girl daydreaming about the future. She had been married five times, and her latest man had not even married her. They just lived together. Her experiences certainly scarred her in emotional ways.

As in any hot, dry part of the world, women would draw their water from the well in the early morning when it was still cool, but not her. She came to the well around lunch time. Perhaps because the women in the town made her feel unworthy or unwelcome. Or maybe she herself felt like she was not worthy to be around the other women of her town.

Then one day Jesus was there. He engaged her in conversation. But not like the other men she had known. He was different. He politely asked her for a drink. He talked about spiritual matters. Imagine her shock and dismay when He told her He knew of her past. He knew how she had lived...how she was living. He knew of her thirst for something better. He did not dismiss her interest in spiritual things. He promised her living water that would quench the thirst in her for something deeper and longer lasting than what she had.

He was the Messiah she had been waiting for. He knew her, and He loved her anyway. He deemed her worthy of saving.

So She Told Everyone In Her Town

The woman immediately went into town and began telling

everyone about the man she had met. She was so excited she even left her water jar back at the well. The crux of her message was that He knew all about her—everything she had ever done. She must have talked about His offer of living water and His claim to be the Messiah. She began asking the others if they thought this man really could be the Christ. And the whole town went out to see Him.

Because of her powerful testimony, many in that town came to believe in Jesus. Then as they heard Jesus talk, even more became believers because of His words.

> ***They said to the woman, "It is no longer because of what you said that we believe, for we have heard for ourselves, and we know that this is indeed the Savior of the world."***
> John 4:42

It still works that way. Your testimony about what Jesus has done in your life will lead people to become followers. But our job is to point them to Jesus...it is always about Jesus, not us. Begin telling people what the Lord has done for you. Then share with them the good news about Jesus so that they, too, may become His followers.

Because Today Is a Day of Good News

It is one of the most graphic stories in all of the Bible. You can read it in 2 Kings 6 and 7, and there are so many things for us to learn from this story, so...

It is a hard world. The capital was under siege, and God's people were in trouble. If you were rich, you could afford to buy a donkey head to eat. That's right...not a donkey, but a donkey head. And that was if you were rich. If you were poor, you spent your few coins to buy dove dung. Not dove, not even dove feathers...but dove dung. How hungry would you have to be to eat bird droppings?

About as hungry as this woman who complained to the

king. She and another mother had agreed to kill and eat the first woman's child one day, and then eat the other woman's child the next. They killed and ate the first child, but the second woman had hidden her child. The king was being asked to make a woman give up her child for a meal.

Donkey head, dove dung, and cannibalism. It was a hard world.

And it is still a hard world today. Natural disasters that destroy property and lives. Hurricanes, earthquakes, tsunamis, tornados, fire, and flood. Bad news from the doctor. Cancer, heart issues, debilitating illnesses that sometimes cannot even be diagnosed. Death, disease, and disaster. It is still a hard world.

So some blame God. The king did. He was so enraged at what was happening that he vowed to chop off the head of Elisha. Why Elisha? Because he was a prophet of God. The king was blaming God.

People still blame God and question God today. Where was God when my child died? Why was my house destroyed? Does God care? Does God hear? This is God's fault. If God is so good, then why is this world so messed up? Mad at God, questioning God, even hating God for what has happened in their world.

But truth is still truth. When the king and his men found Elisha, the prophet spoke truth. In spite of how things looked, God was still in control. Elisha explained that the few coins used to buy dove dung today would buy large quantities of flour or barley the next day. Of course, it sounded unbelievable. In fact, one of the men with the king scoffed at Elisha. He said that even if God opened the floodgates of heaven, that would not happen. Elisha not only said that it would happen, but that this scoffer would see it but not be able to participate in it.

And today we still speak truth into a world that is skeptical about our God. God does reign, His will is going to be done, and He will set things right again. There will be people who will see that day come, but will not get to enjoy it. Truth is truth. God is over all. We speak His praises in this world.

And it got worse. How can it get worse than cannibalism and dove dung? Being a leper in a starving city. There were four lepers begging at the city gates. I cannot imagine how they had survived. Lepers were thought to be incredibly contagious and because leprosy affects the extremities (fingers, nose, ears), it is impossible to disguise. No one would even touch a leper. They obviously could not find work, so most lepers begged. But what do you beg for in a starving city? Do you ask for a tip of the ear of a donkey head? No hope and no future for these guys.

Well, you may have figured it out by now. We are the lepers in this story. How can our world be worse than natural disasters, sickness, and death? Sin. Other people's sins contribute to a world gone wrong. Sexual slavery, alcoholism, violence, theft, and on and on. But it is our own sin that haunts us. Bad choices and poor decisions. Intentional disregard of what we should do. Embracing the things we should not do. Broken relationships. No hope, no peace, and no joy. We believers know what we would be without Jesus. And it is bad. That is why we live forgiven. Loving God for what He did for us. But we know exactly what we would be without Jesus.

Desperate times call for desperate measures. The lepers decided to surrender to the enemy. They had to be aware that they might be killed, but at least it would be quick. And who knew, the enemy might be merciful to them. If they stayed in the city, death was certain. And it would be slow. There was absolutely nowhere else to turn.

That is why we came to Jesus. There is nowhere else to turn for salvation. We get it. We are lost without hope and dead in our sins without Jesus. There are people in your world who are desperate for a different life. They have tried money, pleasure, popularity, and everything the world offers...and nothing works in the long run. But they sense there has to be something better. We know what that something—that Someone—is.

God was at work the whole time. God fooled the Arameans. He caused them to hear the sound of chariots, horses, and a great army. The Arameans decided the king of Israel had hired mercenaries to attack them. They panicked and ran, leaving everything behind in their camp. They left food, livestock, weapons, gold and silver. God had saved His people.

The good news for your world is that Jesus died for their sins so they can be reconciled to God. God raised Jesus from the dead. Death and Satan have been defeated. Satan, death, and sin are powerless over the ones who believe in Jesus. God has acted to save your world.

Held hostage by a beaten enemy. They were eating dove dung, donkey head, and their own children. They did not have to do that. God had defeated their enemy. There was food outside the city. And there was no enemy outside the city. Saved without knowing about it.

Your friends and family without Jesus do not have to live with no hope. Jesus has died, so they can be free. Forgiven of their sins and freed to live a new life. No fear of death. Living with joy, peace, and purpose. Your world is enslaved by an enemy that Jesus has defeated. They can be saved but do not know it.

The lepers found out about it. They went to the enemy camp and there was no one to surrender to because the camp was deserted. They found food and drink in the empty tents. I can only imagine how they must have crammed food into their mouths and guzzled down the wine. And they found gold. There was gold and silver. They were burying it and going from tent to tent to find more. It had to be the greatest day of their lives. They were dead but now alive. Don't you know there was shouting and laughter and singing and praising God among those four lepers?

The day you decided to follow Jesus was the greatest day of your life. Remember how clean and dedicated you felt. We still celebrate our salvation. We meet regularly to celebrate it. We take the body and blood of Christ together in Communion to proclaim our belief in Him. We are the lepers in the deserted camp. God is pouring His blessings out on us. We are blessed above all others. Celebrate, rejoice, and praise God for your salvation.

We are not doing right. I do not know even one of their names, but these lepers are heroes. They could have kept the news of deliverance to themselves. Or set up a really sharp business model to make up for the years of begging. After all, the whole law of supply and demand seems pretty significant here. But they did not. They knew that good news needed to be shared. They realized they had to make a choice. Share this news or punishment would overtake them. They even accepted that if they waited till morning that would be wrong. Life-changing good news has to be shared immediately.

Your world is full of dying people. People who will face judgment without Jesus. People who need what we have. What are the consequences if we keep this to ourselves? Eternity away from God for those who never follow Jesus. And what does it say about us if we hold this secret to ourselves? How can we claim to love God and to love our neighbor as ourselves...yet never tell them the one thing that will change their eternal destiny?

So the king had it checked out. The lepers went back into the city and reported what they had found. The king sent some of his officers to check it out and they found it to be true.

This is exactly what we do by the way we live and serve. We are inviting people to check out the Jesus way. Ready to tell them the good news when they have been attracted by the witness and testimony of seeing our lives and receiving our service. They will find it to be true.

Not everyone ate. Remember the officer who did not believe Elisha. His job was to keep order at the gate when the news was announced. How do you do that in a starving city? He couldn't, of course. In the stampede to get food, the people of the city trampled that man to death.

We cannot control whether or not people believe the good news of Jesus. That is their choice. We can control whether or not they have the opportunity to respond to the news that Jesus died for their sins and God raised Him from the dead so we could have life forever with God. After that, it is their choice.

> ***Then they said to one another, "We are not doing right. This day is a day of good news. If we are silent and wait until the morning light, punishment will overtake us. Now therefore come; let us go and tell the king's household."***
> 2 Kings 7:9

SO WHAT COMES NEXT?

This is the question that I can't answer for you. I can answer it for me, and I can answer for my family. We are going to follow Jesus, and we are going to make followers. I love getting a phone call from my 86-year-old mom asking advice on how to share Jesus with one of her friends. My daughter is still inviting friends in trouble to come with her to church. My son and his wife send me prayer requests for friends and neighbors they are talking to about Jesus.

So here is what I am praying you will do.

Live Forgiven Because You Love God

God has saved you, and you are forgiven through Jesus. Live that way. Be more like Jesus every day. Let the fruit of the Spirit be more evident in your life because you are growing in Christ. Keep putting to death the sins that still want to exist in your life. Love God with all your heart, soul, mind, and strength. People will notice. And they may want to know what it is that makes you different. Your life will be an authentic witness to the Jesus way. Live your story and your message.

Serve Others Because You Love Them

Be a great friend and a good neighbor. Be there for people in need. Serve them in the name of Jesus. Be a friend to the lonely, feed the hungry, care for the sick, be the person people count on. Do these things in the name of Jesus. Be willing to spend your time, money, and energy taking care of people. They will want to know why. That is your opportunity to speak about Jesus. Serving people opens doors for the message of Jesus. It gives you credibility. You will be a living witness for Jesus.

Speak Boldly Because Jesus Told You To...

Followers make followers, and to do that, you must tell others the good news of Jesus. Learn to give God credit for what He does in your life. Be sure and do service in the name of Jesus. Learn to share your story: what God has done in your life. Learn to tell other stories from your community of faith. Share stories from Scripture.

Follow Jesus and make more followers.

Because Jesus said...

And he said to them, "The harvest is plentiful, but the laborers are few. Therefore pray earnestly to the Lord of the harvest to send out laborers into his harvest.

Luke 10:2

And Jesus came and said to them, "All authority in heaven and on earth has been given to me. Go therefore and make disciples of all nations, baptizing them in the name of the Father and of the Son and of the Holy Spirit, teaching them to observe all that I have commanded you. And behold, I am with you always, to the end of the age."

Matthew 28:18-20

So what will you do? The answer is up to you.